D1558210

The MISSOULA MERCANTILE

The MISSOULA MERCANTILE

The Store that Ran an Empire

MINIE SMITH

Published by The History Press
Charleston, SC 29403
www.historypress.net

Copyright © 2012 by Minie Smith
All rights reserved

Front cover: Stylized illustration of the Missoula Mercantile Store. Image no. 001VIII_78-12_170, Archives and Special Collections, Mansfield Library, University of Montana. *Back cover, top left*: Image courtesy of the Audrey Kremis Schultz Collection, 2005.062.157b. Used by Permission. *Back cover, center*: Image no. 001-1_24-22, Archives and Special Collections, Mansfield Library, University of Montana. *Back cover, top*: Image no. 70-0113. Archives and Special Collections, Mansfield Library, University of Montana.

First published 2012

Manufactured in the United States

ISBN 978.1.60949.409.4

Library of Congress CIP data applied for.

Notice: The information in this book is true and complete to the best of our knowledge. It is offered without guarantee on the part of the author or The History Press. The author and The History Press disclaim all liability in connection with the use of this book.

All rights reserved. No part of this book may be reproduced or transmitted in any form whatsoever without prior written permission from the publisher except in the case of brief quotations embodied in critical articles and reviews.

CONTENTS

FOREWORD

History is neither more nor less than biography on a large scale.
—Lamartine

For us, history is the glass through which we may behold the deeds of past ages. Such an age is important to Missoulians. It is the age of the history of an entrepreneurial organization that came to be known as the Missoula Mercantile Company.

This book brings into focus the role this conglomerate company played in the founding and development of Missoula as a city and as part of western Montana.

R.H. Ty Robinson
Former Counsel for the Missoula Mercantile Company

INTRODUCTION

The retail store Bonner & Welch became the Missoula Mercantile Company (MMCo) in 1885 and went on to become the largest department store between Minneapolis and Seattle. This was primarily due to one man, Andrew Hammond, and his relatives from New Brunswick, Canada. The story of the MMCo, Andrew Hammond and the town and county of Missoula remained intertwined years after Hammond's death.

Hammond traced the roots of the Mercantile to 1866, the year Bonner & Welch was formed—six years before he actually was involved with the Mercantile. By the time it finally closed in 2010, some form of the store had been selling merchandise for over 144 years. The Missoula Mercantile itself was sold in 1959 to a larger department store chain. Now, in 2012, the building is prepared for a revival of a different kind. This remarkable story unfolds in the following pages.

The story of the Missoula Mercantile, or "the Merc," is not just the story of a large department store and its decisions to sell a particular line of dresses or shoes, candlesticks and soap; rather, it is the story of one man's empire and vision, as well as that of a father and son and a host of employees who made the local department store chain a success. The store's growth is intertwined with the growth of Missoula itself, a town that started out without streets before dirt ones were made, followed by properly paved roads and sidewalks. Moreover, it is tied to the early development of the fledgling territory of Montana as it struggled with decisions, such as where to establish the state capital and its state university. This progress not only involved inevitable power struggles and bribery but also prompted the store's managers to consider the needs of a community as well as its well-being. The latter is why people remember the Missoula Mercantile with fondness and nostalgia.

Ty Robinson and Gordon Swanson, former employees who both worked at the Missoula Mercantile before 1950, remember much about the old store. Ty recalled how astonished he was at seeing the three thousand pairs of horseshoes in the basement of the store when he started there in 1948. Looking at the Mercatile's eight-hundred-page hardware catalog from 1916, horseshoes were big sellers then and occupied several pages. The Merc also had a special catalog of its best-selling buggy whips, which could be purchased for $0.25 to $1.75 each or by the dozen. Horse and buggy was the way to travel in the early days of the store, and the Merc made sure it catered to all needs. Dennis Sain worked in the toy department in 1958 and remembered a barrel of buggy whips was still in the basement.

The Missoula Mercantile grew to have a reputation for having everything; the company would order anything you wanted if it did not have it in stock (and probably would order several) and did not throw out anything. Jim Meyers, who became the general manager in 1959, commented that in the old days, the Missoula Mercantile had a lot of stock. "There was about $2 million worth of hardware and $700,000 worth of groceries—that's a lot of groceries!" he said.

A few people today still remember the store's manager, C.H. McLeod. Gordon Swanson recalled that when he came back to work in 1946 after the war, C.H. had greeted him, saying, "Glad to see you, Sonny!" and gave him a friendly whack with his walking cane. Meyers's account also had a story of McLeod's cane. Meyers worked in the appliance department selling on commission in the late 1930s, and one day, he was sitting down when McLeod came up and tapped him with the cane, saying something like, "Get up! You made more money than I did last month. Get off your hind end!" Jim had responded, "Well, Mr. McLeod, if you just sold enough appliances, you would have made that kind of money." McLeod had laughed. "He was a nice guy, a great guy," Jim went on.

Today, it is not unusual to find people in Missoula who remember shopping at the store; but if it is the old Merc, the store before 1959, that they recall, then what they remember is the hardware department. The hardware department is most often remembered, especially its creaky wooden floors and its walls full of small drawers containing nuts, bolts and other small hardware items. Many even remember the ladders that ran on rails and allowed employees to access those drawers. Others have different memories.

One customer remembered going to the store in the summertime, when the Merc was cooled by swamp coolers on the roof, and how humid it was. Another remembered the Lionel train at Christmastime, a standard feature of the toy department. And another young customer recalled going to the Merc on a shopping trip with her grandmother after enjoying a "green river milkshake" at the Florence Hotel Café across the street.

This book concentrates on the original store before it was sold in 1959, the store that was the Missoula Mercantile. Hopefully, what follows will give the reader a flavor of the store's fascinating past; given the constraints of time and space, it would be virtually impossible to include all the many details of its complicated history.

So many people have helped me as I tried to pull the story together, and I do appreciate their willingness to share stories and memories of the Merc. I so wish I could thank them all individually. I have tried to accurately relate the stories and information, but of course, all mistakes and misinterpretations remain my own responsibility. I would especially like to mention the following:

Special thanks go to Donna McCrae, archivist at the University of Montana, and her staff, especially Teresa Hamann, who guided my searches, and Mark Fritch, who created scans of the university's photos included in this book. Thanks, too, to Bob Brown and his staff at the Historical Museum at Fort Missoula, for sharing the museum's many Mercantile artifacts, and particularly curator Nicole Webb, who retrieved and photographed some for the book. I am very grateful to the former employees of the Merc and its successors who spoke with me and shared their stories, especially Ty Robinson and Gordon Swanson. A special thanks goes to Ty for writing the foreword to this book and answering my endless questions! Steve McFaddon and Dennis Sain's tour of the empty building gave me an understanding that would not have been possible otherwise. Debbie McConaughey and Ina Swanson brought the credit union's history to life, and Hope Stocksted, Judy Baldizar, Anna Sain and Concetta Whitney gave me insights into the store's more recent history.

Thanks also to Nancy Rice Fritz, who organized a tea party to talk about the old days at the Merc with Meg Rice, Pete Poulis and Dorothy Rades. Mary Pitch, a McLeod descendant, shared many stories, and her wonderful genealogy chart helped me to sort out the intertwining relationships of the five major families involved. Thanks to Dale Johnson, former archivist at the university, not only for his important thesis on Hammond but also for all the encouragement along the way; and to Jim Habeck, for his encouragement and the many relevant articles he passed on. I am very grateful to Stan Cohen for sharing his extensive photographic collection of Missoula and for letting me use some in the book. Robert Wattenburg helped me understand the Hammond connection to the Holy Spirit Church, and Duane Hampton and Dan Flores explained their roles as Hammond professors. It was Dan's graduate student, Greg Gordon, whose recent thesis on A.B. Hammond brought new insights about this complex man.

Thanks to Kim Briggeman for sharing his incredible knowledge of Missoula history; to Jeff Langton for insights about Victor; to Jim Brown for discovering the Grass Valley connection; to Patrice Schwenk for background on St. Michael's Church; to Allan Mathews and Kathryn McKay; and to Chirs and Karen Roholt for interviewing Chris's mother. Thanks also to my cohorts at the Bonner Milltown History Center, for providing me with precious bits of information about the Merc and Bonner and especially for their ongoing support. Thank you Judy Matson for reading through a draft. I am grateful, too, to Pete Goergen of Octagon for his willingness to share access to their building and to Jeff Crouch and Lesley Gilmore of CTA Architects for sharing their discoveries during its restoration process. Thanks to Philip Maechling, the historic preservation officer for Missoula County, for helping me in many ways, from setting up an interview with Ty Robinson to sharing information about early Missoula. But none of this would have been possible without the love and support of my husband, Alan McQuillan, who has lived with the project for its many months and has untiringly helped me in endless ways, from computer and photographic technicalities, to taking pictures of the Merc and sharing them in the book, to helping me straighten out the text to make it more readable.

Minie Smith
May 2012

Chapter One

THE COMING OF THE MISSOULA MERCANTILE

Leaving a Tough Town

The year was 1866. A dusty crossroad in western Montana marked the site of a new community that would soon contain a dozen or more log houses, two stores and a sawmill. Missoula Mills (or simply Missoula as it would soon be known) had just moved four miles east from where it began as Hell Gate Ronde (short for rendezvous), a place described as a "tough town with an average population of twelve," tough no doubt due to the number of shootings and hangings that occurred there. Between 1863 and 1864, there were some ten deaths, none of which was naturally occurring. The narrow canyon of Hell Gate to the east was named for the site's numerous confrontations between the Salish Indians and the invading Blackfeet from the Plains, fur trappers and explorers and others who traversed the trail through it. To the west, the lands flattened out, the result of Glacial Lake Missoula and its catastrophic floodwaters emptying over twelve thousand years ago, leaving the lands suitable for farming.

Two enterprising traders, Christopher P. Higgins and Frank L. Worden, had founded the community of Hell Gate in 1860, establishing a trading post there because of its proximity to the valleys south and north of the settlement and its location on the east–west Mullan Road, which was under construction as a military road between Fort Benton on the Missouri and Walla Walla, Washington, adjacent to the Columbia River. The post, called

Salish teepees at Hell Gate Canyon. *No. 83-0040, Archives and Special Collections, Mansfield Library, University of Montana.*

Worden & Company, was also strategically located between the Flathead Indian Agency at Jocko and Fort Owen in the Bitterroot Valley to the south. Worden and Higgins's store quickly became an important stopping place. Today, Worden & Company is recognized as the oldest general merchandising store in western Montana. But it was not to stay in Hell Gate for long.

Hell Gate was declared the seat of Missoula County in 1865, Missoula being a huge county in what was then Washington Territory. The county "courthouse" was Worden's store. A Jesuit mission, St. Michael's, had also been established at Hell Gate in 1863, under Father Grassi, the superior at St. Ignatius Mission located forty miles to the north on the Flathead Indian Reservation. St. Michael was the saint who barricaded the gates of Hell.

Gold was discovered in nearby Gold Creek in 1861 and in Bannack in 1862, and Higgins and Worden quickly realized that the miners would need food, lumber and other commodities. They were determined to be the suppliers. However, lack of sufficient water power at Hell Gate caused Higgins and Worden to dismantle and move their store about four miles east to take advantage of the stronger flow in nearby Rattlesnake Creek, where, in 1866, they built and operated a sawmill, followed by a gristmill for flour the next year. The town soon followed. It was first called Missoula Mills and was later shortened to Missoula. The building of another Jesuit mission at Frenchtown, eleven miles to the west in 1864, and the reopening of St. Mary's Mission to the south in the Bitterroot Valley in 1866 had replaced any immediate need to move St. Michael's. The church did not actually move to Missoula until 1873, when the Roman Catholic Sisters of Providence opened a hospital there. This, the first church for white settlers in Montana, has subsequently been restored and is now found on the grounds of Missoula County's Historical Museum.

Most users of the store were just passing through and were anxious to get to the gold fields as quickly as possible. This was especially true after more gold was discovered near Kootenai to the northwest, and hundreds streamed there. Hell Gate and its successor, Missoula Mills, were initially part of Washington Territory. As boundaries changed, they became part of Idaho Territory and, finally, part of Montana when that territory was created in 1864. Nothing seemed permanent, but an endless stream of people came through looking for opportunities to get rich somewhere.

Bonner & Welch: The Second Store

Also sensing opportunity were Edward L. Bonner and Daniel J. Welch, traders to the Indians. Bonner had been wholesaling goods by taking pack trains to small stores in the mining camps and, for a time, ran the ferry across Idaho's Kootenai River in a place still known as Bonner's Ferry. Then, in 1866, the two men brought a supply train of merchandise on 125 pack animals and opened a new store in Missoula Mills, calling it Bonner & Welch and soon adding Richard A. Eddy as a clerk. The log cabin store was on West Front Street, in a small space near the later sites of both the Gem Theater and the Florence Hotel Pigeon-Hole parking lot. They quickly became a presence in the new town. The part of Front Street that wound through the town was called Mullan Road, and before long, Bonner and Welch were supplying goods all over western Montana. By the end of the first year, the two men reportedly had an inventory of $16,000 in goods. This was a fair amount of money in a place where the primary currency

Missoula, M. T., 186

Bought of **BONNER & WELCH,**

Wholesale and Retail Dealers in

DRY GOODS, GROCERIES, LIQUORS, BOOTS, SHOES, ETC., ETC.

ALSO KEEP ON HAND A CHOICE ASSORTMENT OF

California and Oregon Goods.

Receipt from Bonner & Welch store, 1869. *No. 76-0056, Archives and Special Collections, Mansfield Library, University of Montana.*

was gold dust. Like Worden & Company, Bonner & Welch sold general merchandise and was both a wholesale and retail merchant. They built a corral opposite the store for the pack mules out of willows that were growing along the riverbank. The story, told over one hundred years later, was that the mules had to be guarded at night from young Indian boys who reached the corral by swimming the river and would then ride off on a mule and make it swim back farther down the river.

Richard Eddy, Bonner & Welch's clerk, also opened a branch store in Bear Gulch, forty miles to the east of Missoula and also on the Mullan Road near the gold mines at Bear Creek. Housing the store in a tent and supplying it from Missoula by pack train kept operating costs low. When the gold mining opportunities dried up, the tent would be packed and moved to any new opportunity. Eddy closed his branch store in 1868 and opened one in Walla Walla, Washington, and then closed it and opened yet another in Frenchtown in 1870. This location was just eleven miles from Missoula but closer to the mines at Cedar Creek where gold had been discovered in 1869. At one time, there were ten thousand people at Cedar Creek, miners vying for the more than $1 million worth of gold that would ultimately be taken out.

Richard Eddy, clerk at Bonner & Welch. *No. 88-0017, Archives and Special Collections, Mansfield Library, University of Montana.*

Missoula's Ideal Location

Missoula was ideally situated for commerce, as Higgins and Worden had been the first to recognize. It was not only located at or near the conjunction of five river valleys but was also on the now firmly established Mullan Military Road. This road, in part following the old trail of the Salish Indians to the buffalo grounds on the plains of the Missouri River, had reached Missoula by 1860. The total 652 miles was more or less completed by 1862, and although it was intended for military use, it was never used for that purpose. Instead, the road provided the needed overland freight connection from the Missouri River to the Columbia River by linking Fort Benton (the farthest point steamboats could navigate on the Missouri) to Walla Walla, Washington. It was primarily used by gold miners and, later, was used by homesteaders. It is estimated that two thousand people, six thousand horses, five thousand cattle and eighty-three wagons used it in its first year.

In 1862–63, however, fewer than 500 people were actually living in what would become Montana Territory, with Missoula County's population (not including the Indians) comprising merely 69 men and 8 women. Missoula became the new county seat in 1866, replacing Hell Gate, which most people had vacated, and taxes were assessed and collected for the first time. Records show there were fourteen homes. The 1870 census showed Missoula County with 2,554 whites, 2,084 of whom were males. They were largely farmers, but there was significant variety in their occupations, from prospectors to lumber manufacturers to a butcher and a baker and even a couple of musicians and stage players to supplement the expected western town jobs of saloonkeeper, mule packer or stage driver. The miners tended not to stay.

For the most part, these people were dependent on outside supplies; the majority of goods had to be imported. Prices could fluctuate wildly. Nails or bacon might be as much as one dollar a pound and then suddenly drop to twenty-five cents a pound if several freighters arrived at the same time with the same commodities. Freight costs were high, from fifteen to forty cents a pound according to John Beadle (writing in 1866) because of the long distances from the supply centers. Still, Beadle reasoned, given that the freight was the same, even if a pound of white sugar cost twenty cents and a pound of brown sugar was only ten, people came to demand the better items. "The difference," said Beadle, "was not worth calculating about away up in Montana." The bottom line was that there was money to be made by both freighters and store owners in supplying the miners and the fledgling farm communities. There were difficulties nonetheless.

The Mullan Road, although initially well financed and built, fell into disrepair a few short years after completion, and freighters did not find it easily usable, especially its western portion. Moreover, Fort Benton on the Missouri at the road's eastern terminus could only be used part of the year due to low water at other times. On average, river steamers did not arrive at Fort Benton until mid-May, and the season only lasted until July, sometimes through August if it was a wet year. Nevertheless, early records show that Frank Worden supplied the store with freight coming from Fort Benton as early as 1862. From the other direction, travel from San Francisco had the added necessity of getting across the Continental Divide, an impossibility in the winter. So in spite of its problems, the preferred route was from Fort Benton, at least until 1869.

It was the arrival of the transcontinental railroads that changed the shipping routes. When the Union Pacific reached Corinne, Utah, on the shore of the Great Salt Lake, it quickly became the major shipping point for destinations in Montana in 1869, even though it still took up to fourteen days of freighting to reach Missoula. In 1870, Henry Walker in *The Wagonmasters* relates that there was one week in which 276,138 pounds were sent on to Montana, including 51,580 pounds to Helena (where gold had been discovered in 1864 in Last Chance Gulch). By 1880, a branch line off the Union Pacific followed the freighters' route directly to Butte, Montana, encouraged by the development of copper mining there around 1875. The Northern Pacific Railroad reached Helena in 1883 with the connecting spike laid at Gold Creek sixty miles east of Missoula in September of that year. This gave direct access east and west without the need to travel north from Utah. The railroads continued to play a significant role in the evolving story of Missoula and its soon-to-be store, the Missoula Mercantile.

E.L. Bonner & Company

Daniel Welch withdrew from the partnership with Bonner in 1871 (although he did subsequently open his own grocery store in Missoula), selling his interest to Richard Eddy, and the store was now called E.L. Bonner & Company. The story might have ended there had not a lanky, ambitious young man named Andrew Bernoni Hammond wandered into the Missoula crossroads from the west in about 1870. Originally from New Brunswick, Canada, Hammond had left home at sixteen and, following his brother George, headed across the border into the States, lumbering in Maine and Pennsylvania and then relocating to the West. He had tried mining and many other small jobs before landing in Missoula as a clerk in the small retail store that George White still ran in Hell Gate (by then, only a few buildings and people were remaining in the town). Both Hammond (as clerk of the store) and White (as retail merchant) appear on the 1870 census, the first census for the new Montana Territory. Under the column indicating value of personal property, Hammond recorded $500; most of his contemporaries entered nothing in that column. Perhaps he was already envisioning future investments. White died soon thereafter in 1871, and although Hammond stayed on to help Mrs. White close out the store, Hammond's brief merchandising experience seemed just one more in a string of unrelated jobs until Richard Eddy offered him the clerk's job at Eddy and Bonner's store in 1872.

Eddy and Bonner's relationship began to alter in the next few years, particularly after the addition of Hammond. Bonner was initially the active partner and was well suited for this task. He had grown up in New York City and had gained merchandising experience at Lord and Taylor, the major department store established there in 1826. Hammond had found he liked merchandising and that he was good at it. After 1876, Richard Eddy chose to become less involved in the day-to-day management of the store, leaving that to Bonner and the new clerk, Andrew Hammond. Eddy did remain financially involved as the store evolved into the Missoula Mercantile.

Edward L. Bonner. *Photograph mtg0000894 in Jack L. Demmons/Bonner School Photographs, Archives and Special Collections, Mansfield Library, University of Montana.*

Another Name: Eddy, Hammond & Company

Adjusting to this new situation, the store was reorganized in 1876, and Hammond became a partner in the renamed store, Eddy Hammond & Company. For a time, Hammond and Bonner worked hand in hand, slowly changing the direction of the store. Bonner moved to Deer Lodge, eighty-fives miles east of Missoula, where he opened a store, again named E.L. Bonner & Company, and purchased goods for both Deer Lodge and Missoula stores. The two stores shared a warehouse in Deer Lodge. Bonner traveled frequently to San Francisco to purchase new lines of goods coming in by train and sea from the East Coast. Hammond traveled to Helena, which was being supplied with goods coming overland via Fort Benton. Before long, they expanded the goods they were selling from dry goods, clothing and boots to ladies' fancy apparel and groceries. In addition to the main store, they still made use of pack trains to supply many of the nearby farming and mining communities adjacent to Missoula.

Bonner's personal focus, however, was changing. Deer Lodge was adjacent to Butte, a town that was expanding fast, growing in ten years from a few hundred people to over five thousand by 1880, primarily due to the rapid development of copper mining. Bonner soon had a store there as well. This meant that more of the responsibility of the Missoula store then fell to Hammond, who was not reticent in taking up the slack.

Hammond at this time also bought livestock that he kept at Flathead Lake nearly one hundred miles north of Missoula. Although his ranching adventure would not prove long term, Dale Johnson, in his PhD thesis in 1976 on A.B. Hammond, credits this experience with giving him an understanding of the financial needs of ranchers, details that might otherwise have escaped

Illustration of Eddy Hammond & Company on Higgins Avenue and Front Street, 1882. *Private collection.*

him. The seasonal ebbs and flows of farm and ranch finances are often inconsistent with urban demands, something Hammond incorporated in his merchandising strategy when selling grain and farm equipment to farmers and ranchers in subsequent years. But who was this man, A.B. Hammond? For that part of the story, we need to return to Canada.

The Early Andrew Hammond

Andrew Bernoni Hammond had already come a long way from his beginnings in New Brunswick by the time he reached Missoula. He had been born in 1848, the second son of Andrew Bernoni Hammond and Glorianna Coombes, and grew up in the small town of St. Leonard, which was named for his grandfather, Leonard Coombes. The town lay just north of the St. John River in the county of Madawaska, New Brunswick, and was just across the river from the state of Maine, a boundary only recently determined by the Asburton Treaty of 1842. In fact, Andrew's uncle, William Cook Hammond, who had settled on the south side of the river, found himself living in Maine after the treaty. He liked it so much that he stayed and became a U.S. citizen.

Andrew (or A.B. as he is sometimes referred to) was a descendant of the aunt of William Penn, the Quaker who founded Pennsylvania. Penn's family started out in Massachusetts and had followed the British Loyalists to Nova Scotia and eventually to the predominately French New Brunswick, where they were one of the few Anglophone families, the area having been established by the French as Acadia.

After the death of Sarah Coombes, Andrew Sr.'s first wife, he moved next door to his father-in-law in St. Leonard Parish and then married Sarah's sister, Glorianna, in 1837. Glorianna gave birth to six children. Her husband was well respected in the community and, being able to speak both English and French, was an asset to both Anglo and Acadian communities. Unfortunately, he died in 1854 when Andrew was just six, and Andrew's grandfather assumed responsibility for him and his siblings. Early on, their grandfather had them helping with the farm work. The four boys—George, Andrew, Fred and Henry—worked hard, but they also attended school. Andrew started at age eleven and was known to love books and history and also had a special interest in Napoleon. He was greatly influenced by his

Andrew Bernoni Hammond as a young man. *No. 84-0075, Archives and Special Collections, Mansfield Library, University of Montana.*

grandfather Leonard's Protestant work ethic and his example in using family members to run various business interests, including the sawmill previously run by his father. Leonard died in 1854, and his brother, William, who had done very well in the lumber business in Maine, became the family patriarch. His success must also have had an influence on the young Andrew.

Shortly thereafter, George and Andrew left the New Brunswick farm, lured by the discovery of gold in Colorado, and were only slowed by the need to make a living on the way. They worked for some time in the Maine woods, eventually heading south to Pennsylvania as the timber demands changed. White pine, which had been the desired species, had all but been cut out, so like other loggers, they followed the new timber opportunities out west.

By 1867, George and Andrew had gotten as far as St. Joseph, Missouri, but having missed the train for Colorado and hearing of gold deposits in Montana, the brothers instead boarded a steamboat on the Missouri River that was bound for Fort Benton. Since the discovery of gold, men were rushing to get to Montana. Boats heavily loaded with supplies, food, clothing and mining equipment were headed upriver. The boats carried furs and gold dust (estimated to be about 1,225 tons in 1867) on the return trip. Business was booming, but the trip was slow. Andrew, tired of the crawling pace of the steamboat as it navigated the ever-changing and meandering channel of the Missouri River, struck out on his own without his brother when the boat stopped at Fort Peck, three hundred miles shy of Fort Benton. He spent the winter chopping wood (for the voracious needs of the steamboats), avoiding Indians (who were understandably upset at the huge influx of boats and men invading their territory) and shooting wolves (for their pelts) for the fur traders Durfee and Peck. He not only managed to survive but also saved some money and surprised his brother by turning up one day in the saloon in Fort Benton.

The brothers journeyed together again, stopping briefly in Hell Gate before landing at the Pope and Talbot's Puget Sound Lumber Mill in Washington, where they were both given jobs. The mill recognized the experience of men from New Brunswick who were known to be hard workers and familiar with the lumber trade. This stint in the mill plus living in a mill town gave Andrew valuable experience, but gold still called to him, and he quit the mill after eighteen months and headed to Cedar Creek, Montana, near Hell Gate to work in the mines. As had been his poor luck before, he arrived too late. Being close to Hell Gate, he continued on to there. It was in the spring of 1870 when he met up with George White, who just happened to also be from New Brunswick. This was to be a fortuitous meeting for both of them.

Chapter Two

THE GROWTH OF MISSOULA

Eddy Hammond & Company Takes Off

Missoula was a quickly erected frontier town that was made up of log buildings. But Missoula was changing and growing. By 1872, there were, according to Missoula historian Alan Matthews, sixty-six occupied buildings, but more than half had been built since 1869. Among these were two hotels and a carpenter shop, two blacksmith shops and two wholesale stores with "well assorted stocks." The greatest feature of the new town, as historian Leeson noted in 1894, was Worden & Company's flour mill and sawmill. "The sawmill has a capacity of two thousand feet per day and the flouring mill, a capacity of four hundred sacks in twenty-four hours," Leeson wrote. "It was finished in November 1867."

Soon thereafter, Worden & Company moved to a new building at the corner of Higgins Avenue and Main Street. This time, the company did not build a log structure but a solid building in what would become known as the Brick Block, which would also include the Missoula National Bank in the back of the building by 1873, as well as Jacob Reinhard's Hardware and Saddlery and J.P. Reinhard's Groceries and Liquor. A bridge across the Missoula River was completed in 1873, and there was a $25 fine for riding or walking faster than a walk or a $100 fine for moving cows in groups greater than ten.

First Higgins Bridge, 1873. *No. 70-0107, Archives and Special Collections, Mansfield Library, University of Montana.*

Between 1872 and 1876, A.B. Hammond appeared less focused on the operation of Eddy Hammond & Company (E.H. & Company) than trying other ventures. He spent the winter of 1871–72 at Flathead Lake, where his uncle, Valentine Coombes, known as Uncle Walt, was the postmaster from 1872 to 1875, having himself migrated from New Brunswick. This is the period during which Andrew tried ranching in a joint venture with his brother Fred, who had also moved from St. Leonard. Hammond also tried being a medicinal salesman, selling get-well remedies from a wagon in the Bitterroot. He was slowed down by a bout of undefined illness, which would reoccur the rest of his life. By 1876, however, he had recovered and settled back as clerk with renewed vigor and proved prepared to take on the responsibilities of partner in a growing merchandising firm.

After the mines played out, men either drifted away or settled in around Missoula, taking up farming. Thus, Missoula began to have a small permanent population. Like its competitor, Worden & Company, E.H. & Company was poised to take advantage of this situation. But unlike Worden & Company, which concentrated on Missoula, E.H. & Company organized its permanent Missoula store using the same methods it had used to supply the mining camps, with branch stores supplied by a central store, only the branches would be designed to be permanent instead of small branch outlets in tents.

Hammond began expanding E.H. & Company in 1877 by opening a branch in Stevensville in the Bitterroot Valley after acquiring partial ownership of the well-known house of Jeremiah Fahey. What appealed most to the Bitterroot Valley residents about this new arrangement was that E.H. & Company had decided that prices would be the same in Stevensville as they were in Missoula; people would not have to come into Missoula to get the lower prices. This was a new strategy but one that would serve E.H. & Company well in the future.

In Missoula, Hammond and Bonner, who by then were the primary operators of E.H. & Company, soon found the location of their twenty- by ten-foot log cabin store on West Front Street too small and set about moving to a bigger and more visible site on the corner of East Front and Higgins. The new building would be twelve times larger (thirty feet by eighty-five feet) and would have a granite foundation. Stonemasons Murphy and Myers from Helena were given that job. This suggested the new E.H. & Company store, like Worden & Company, was to be permanent, unusual for businesses at this time, when the philosophy was to "get in and get rich and get out." Like the old log building, the new one faced Front Street, and much of the Higgins Avenue side was a solid brick wall, which would be used later for advertising, as Higgins became the primary retail street.

The *Missoulian* newspaper, which itself only started in 1871 (as the *Missoula and Cedar Creek Pioneer*), was glad to report the expansion of a new business, and it regularly noted the building progress in 1877. "In March the ground was excavated," reported the paper. "By June the walls were up to the top of the windows, and then the roof put on and the business was able to move in on October 19th." This would be only the first of several improvements to the store that would be made in the next few years. Parts of the original foundation are still visible today in the basement of the old store. An awning provided shade over a wooden sidewalk on both the Front Street and the Higgins Avenue sides, and people readily gathered there. The name of the building was displayed on the front side at Front Street, which also had a false front that rose above the roof.

In 1877, there were other buildings appearing in Missoula. Fort Missoula opened to the west of town and was established to protect the citizens of Missoula from a perceived Indian threat. But as it turned out, the soldiers actually had little to do. Just after the soldiers arrived, however, one incident did take place that concerned the Nez Perce Tribe and, by coincidence, related to E.H. & Company. It occurred in June 1877, during the building process. At that time, some seven hundred Nez Perce were being moved against their will to a reservation in southern Idaho by U.S. troops. Missoula residents, nervous after hearing of Custer's loss at the Battle of Big Horn the previous year, took shelter behind E.H. & Company's stone foundations from what

Eddy Hammond & Company store becomes the Missoula Mercantile Store. *No. 70-0113, Archives and Special Collections, Mansfield Library, University of Montana.*

they feared would be an attack by the Indians. According to Edward Boos, future head of public relations for the Missoula Mercantile, the foundations were thought to be the most defensible place in town. However, the Nez Perce, under Chief Joseph, wished to bypass Missoula peaceably and took to the mountains over the Lolo Trail, a traditional Indian route. They not only bypassed Missoula but also effectively bypassed Captain Charles Rowan and his soldiers, who had been sent out from Fort Missoula to stop the Indians at a place now known as Fort Fizzle. Construction of E.H. & Company resumed. (The fate of the Nez Perce was, unfortunately, not so peaceful; they were to meet disaster at the Battle of the Big Hole by August that year.)

The next improvement for the store came in 1878, when a new sidewalk was installed on the Higgins Avenue side and a twenty- by thirty-foot fireproof office was added in the rear. And in 1880, E.H. & Company purchased land to "erect a large barn and shed for the accommodation of freight teams," according to the *Missoulian*. "They will have room for probably 30 head of horses and 25 tons of hay." By 1880, E.H. & Company was generating $15,000 a month in sales. It had become the dominant wholesale-retail company in Missoula, easily surpassing Worden & Company, much to the dismay of its two founders.

It was clear that there was a rivalry between Hammond and Higgins that would be fought in other arenas; they disagreed over the location of the new bridge over the river and then over Missoula's bank. Worden & Company continued despite Hammond's best efforts to shut it down. In 1886, Worden & Company merged with Murphy, Hart and Company, which also sold general merchandise, but by 1902, the store had been reduced to simply being a grocery store. F.L. Worden and C.P. Higgins died shortly afterward (1887 and 1889, respectively). Nevertheless, the rivalry that had existed between Hammond and Higgins would continue into the next generation.

Now that Andrew Hammond was spending more time overseeing the expanding store, he came to realize that he would need help. He turned to his family in New Brunswick, knowing they would recommend men who were reliable and hardworking. Thus began a pattern repeated many times in his business career: recruiting relatives and people recommended by relatives to manage his business interests. It was a successful endeavor, and for the most part, these men willingly devoted their lives to the various Hammond interests. The first to arrive was Thomas Hatheway in 1878 from New Brunswick. He would be the company bookkeeper and clerk. He was adept at doing a number of other tasks, including making deliveries from the store, which he did at night with a wheelbarrow. According to a story, he reportedly said that he did this at night, as he could not tip his hat when holding on to the handles of the wheelbarrow. Hatheway later became involved in Hammond's first major real estate–lumber venture as assistant manager of the Montana Improvement Company (MIC). His name would also appear as one of the incorporators of the new Bonner sawmill, the Big Blackfoot Milling Company, which would be owned by the MIC by 1891.

In 1880, the man who was to be the major player in Hammond's future empire came to Missoula, at the recommendation of Hammond's sister Mary. This man was a nephew of Andrew's named Charles Herbert McLeod. The tale of McLeod's adventures in getting to Montana was believable for the Wild West of that time. He traveled to Bear Canyon, near Bozeman, by train and then took a stage to Missoula, having to spend the night on the way in Dillon, where he was given a table to sleep on in a warehouse. He was reportedly unable to wake up the man next to him the following morning and only later discovered that he had been dead

Charles Herbert McLeod as a young man. *No. 88-0042, Archives and Special Collections, Mansfield Library, University of Montana.*

and awaiting a funeral. The rest of McLeod's stage ride to Missoula was apparently uneventful.

McLeod did many jobs the first year, including chopping wood and clerking. He only got half a day off for Christmas, and he worked all the other holidays. Before long, Hammond would make him store manager and deeply involve him in Hammond's growing number of enterprises.

Bringing the Relatives

By the early 1880s, much of Hammond's immediate family had migrated to Missoula or the surrounding area. Hammond had indicated that there was

A.B. Hammond and family. *No. 88-0042, Archives and Special Collections, Mansfield Library, University of Montana.*

opportunity and good wages, and there seemed to be little to hold them back in New Brunswick. His brother George was already in the Missoula area, having journeyed out west with Andrew; Fred and William Henry (who went by Henry) followed later. By 1886, his mother, Glorianna, had also come with his sisters: Sarah, who had married Charles E. Beckwith, and Mary, who had married George W. Fenwick also from Canada. These families, particularly as the generations progressed, intermarried: the names of Hammond, Coombes, Fenwick, McLeod and Beckwith would become the basis of Hammond's economic grasp of Missoula and, later, of his lumber enterprises on the West Coast.

Andrew himself tightened the circle by marrying Florence Abbott, Richard Eddy's sister-in-law. The marriage took place in 1880. Florence had grown up in Portland, Oregon, and had come to live with Richard and his wife, Edwina, in Missoula. Andrew and Florence would go on to have six children: Edwina, Florence, Richard, Leonard, Grace and Daisy. Richard died in 1911 of tuberculosis and Daisy never married, but all of the other Hammond children did.

Andrew and C.H. McLeod's close relationship was the key to the success of Hammond's operations. It was clear from the beginning that E.H. & Company and its successor, the Missoula Mercantile, were more than department stores, a fact that would ultimately affect Hammond's relationship with a lot of Missoulians.

Andrew and Herb maintained their strong relationship all their lives despite the distance. After Andrew moved to California, the two families frequently visited each other. Hammond tried to persuade McLeod to move to California to manage his affairs from there, but McLeod always steadfastly refused. Communication then was mostly by letter, and A.B.'s letters were usually addressed "Dear Herb" or "My dear Sir," while C.H.'s were always formal, reading "Dear Mr. Hammond," which might reflect merely the formal time in which they were living. Although Hammond was the boss, C.H. was not afraid to stand up to him or disagree on some point of business, and he often did. But for the most part, he loyally carried out Hammond's wishes. In these first few years, however, McLeod was still learning and did not have major responsibilities in Hammond's ventures apart from the store.

The Coming of the Railroad

The population of Missoula and the surrounding area was growing, primarily due to new farmers, and as one early economist noted, the people were "living in anticipation of the railroad." The Panic of 1873 had stopped the Northern Pacific Railroad (Northern Pacific) literally in its tracks, and it was not until 1881 that construction was rolling again after Northern Pacific underwent a complete reorganization. As incentive, the five "transcontinental" railroads had been given some 100 million acres of the public domain by Congress to engage in this major and risky undertaking of taking the trains west. Of this, the Northern Pacific was awarded fully 47 percent of the total. As most of this land was heavily forested, Northern Pacific consequently became a prime operator in the lumber business. This kind of encouragement succeeded, and the Northern Pacific completed its transcontinental route from St. Paul, Minnesota, to Seattle, striking the golden spike September 8, 1883.

In Missoula, both the Worden-Higgins side and the Bonner-Hammond-Eddy side realized how important it would be to Missoula's future to make sure that the Northern Pacific did not bypass the town, for that would have assured the demise of Missoula. Higgins and Worden offered their land in the center of town to the Northern Pacific, which they surmised would nicely serve not only the station but also the roundhouse and rail yards. Hammond had his eyes on bigger fish and managed to convince the Northern Pacific to award E.H. & Company (that is, its partners Hammond, Bonner and Eddy) a contract to supply Northern Pacific with all it needed to build the track between the Little Blackfoot River and the Thompson River, located 175 miles west. This involved not only clearing the right of way and supplying the ties for the track and lumber for bridges but also food and clothing for the men building the track. Thus, E.H. & Company was building markets for its store, markets that if it played its cards correctly could later be turned into branch stores once the towns developed alongside the tracks. For the moment, it was content to set up tent stores since it lacked mills to turn the trees it cut into lumber needed for railroad building. It is said that Hammond took the chief engineer for the Northern Pacific on a visit to Flathead Lake and returned home with a signed contract, much to the resentment of Higgins and Worden, although Northern Pacific did take the offer of their land for the depot as well. McLeod confirmed Hammond's role in a letter he wrote in 1940: "While Mr. Bonner may have signed the papers, the contract was made by Mr. Hammond."

Bonner immediately went east to buy machinery to run a sawmill, and Eddy took men up the Blackfoot River to find a suitable mill site. Lumber mills at that time were largely temporary and were built so that they could be moved once the available timber nearby had been cut. As it turned out, the mill they would build at Bonner near the confluence of the Missoula (now Clark Fork) and Blackfoot Rivers would be a permanent mill. They realized that there was a huge demand for wood; not only was the railroad building track, but they foresaw that the copper mines in Butte, owned by Marcus Daly and William Andrews Clark, needed a seemingly endless supply of mine props or stulls to keep mining operations running.

The considerable acreage that the railroads had been awarded, which was carved out of the public domain, was interspersed with the remaining public domain in a checkerboard ownership pattern. The key problem here was that none of these lands had yet been surveyed; the government didn't know exactly where its lands or the railroad boundaries were. Hammond, Eddy, Bonner and M.J. Connell, Bonner's partner in

Picture of the basement of the Missoula Mercantile, where the cigars and liquor department was, late 1880s. *No. 001-viii_78-10_142, Archives and Special Collections, Mansfield Library, University of Montana.*

Deer Lodge, organized a new corporation in August 1882, called the Montana Improvement Company. Also included were Marcus Daly, who was developing Butte's rich copper resources, and Washington Dunn, Northern Pacific's construction superintendent. Although it would later vigorously deny it in court, MIC appeared ready to take advantage of this vast lumber resource–extraction opportunity in any way it could. To give it maximum flexibility to operate, the corporation was set up to do business not only in Montana but also in Washington and Idaho. The deal it worked out with Northern Pacific ran for twenty years and was to supply the railroad with timber for a distance of 925 miles, from Miles City, Montana, to Walla Walla, Washington. MIC would have the right to cut timber from Northern Pacific's lands and along the railroad right of way for all of the 925 miles. Needless to say, it was a lucrative contract. By the next year, MIC already had several "portable" mills working and was planning the permanent mill in Bonner, having also taken over the mills of E.H. & Company, which had four to five small operating sawmills, including the nearby ones at Bonita and Clinton. By 1883, all the mills owned by E.H. & Company were taken over by MIC.

This contract was intricately tied to E.H. & Company's growing store on the corner of Front and Higgins. A huge increase in goods was needed, and thus, the additional space was required, particularly warehouse space. Having capital, E.H. & Company was able to pay cash for large quantities of items. In 1880, the store was almost doubled in size with a dry goods store (thirty-five feet by one hundred feet), a hardware store (twenty feet by one hundred feet) and liquor and cigar store (twenty-six feet by one hundred feet), and in 1883, plans were made to add a second story with more space for merchandise and also to house the office of the MIC. By autumn, E.H. & Company had eighteen clerks and bookkeepers. It also established a number of tent stores along the railroad construction line, stores that came and went according to need. And because of its close relationship with the Northern Pacific, MIC also negotiated lower rates on shipping its goods on the line. Bypassing Worden & Company, E.H. & Company was now the largest employer after the railroad, and it dominated the wholesale and retail trade in groceries, clothing and hardware for most of western Montana. In 1880, according to its records, its wholesale business was $180,000, with an additional $125,000 retail, and by 1882, wholesale had increased to $450,000. Over the next few years, the store bought land and then built warehouses around Missoula, all while continuing to expand the main store.

The Missoula Mercantile Is Born

But for all its seemingly unstoppable growth, the Montana Improvement Company would not last long. Correctly suspecting that the government might investigate its lumber-cutting practices for ignoring ownership boundaries while vigorously denying it, Hammond developed a strategy to diversify his investments so that evidence of his investments was not as obvious. He thus began to spread out the ownership interests of these companies among his trusted relatives and employees. Thus, E.H. & Company disappeared in 1885, and a new company called the Missoula Mercantile Company (MMCo) was formed. The name E.H. & Company would continue as a subsidiary of the Missoula Mercantile by being set up

Employees of the Missoula Mercantile Company, 1885. *No. 70-105, Archives and Special Collections, Mansfield Library, University of Montana.*

Photograph of inventory being brought in by horse, 1885. Note the brick wall facing Higgins Avenue with advertising. *No. 001-viii_78-12_168, Archives and Special Collections, Mansfield Library, University of Montana.*

as a Delaware Corporation (which was favorable for tax advantages), and it would last until 1953, the year it was finally subsumed into the MMCo. Another new company was formed—the Missoula Real Estate Association (MREA), which would buy and sell land in the growing town of Missoula. In 1888, MREA built a hotel opposite the Missoula Mercantile, and Hammond named it the Florence Hotel, after his wife. Later, the South Missoula Land Company would be formed to buy and sell real estate in undeveloped land south of the river in Missoula. The Montana Improvement Company then morphed into the Blackfoot Milling Company, with William Henry Hammond at the helm. According to the *Missoula County Times*, all of this occurred while the "government stumpage agents [were] abroad in the land."

Although the lumber mill in Bonner would be reincorporated several more times in the next couple of years under new names (Blackfoot Milling and Manufacturing Company, Big Blackfoot Milling Company and then the Big Blackfoot Milling and Manufacturing Company) to try to thwart these government investigations, the Missoula Mercantile name remained. Initially, MMCo consisted of A.B. Hammond, president; Richard Eddy, vice-president; and John M. Keith (who also married one of Hammond's nieces and C.H.'s sister-in-law, Hattie), secretary and treasurer. C.H. McLeod replaced Hammond as the store's general manager. The government cases (criminal and civil) against Hammond were to continue well into the next century, and although he was accused of cutting well over $1 million worth of trees illegally on public lands, Hammond ended up paying a meager fine of just over $17,000.

Chapter Three

MANAGING MORE THAN THE MISSOULA MERCANTILE

McLeod and Hammond

The reorganization of E.H. & Company into the Missoula Mercantile Company (MMCo) occurred in August 1885. The new corporation had a capital of $250,000.

The *Missoulian* reported:

> *The Missoula Mercantile Company open for business with ample capital, paying cash for all goods, and are therefore in position to sell on as close margin as any house west of the Missouri River...During the nine years this enterprising firm has done business in Missoula, they have built up probably a more extensive trade than any other firm in Missoula, several years showing sales of over one million dollars per year. The object of forming corporations and taking in employees as associates is that the old firm have outside business of such magnitude as to require much of their time and attention and to give their tried and worthy employees an opportunity to invest their earnings where it will do them the most good. We prophesy prosperity for the new corporation.*

There were actually only 4 shares of the $100 shares offered to employees out of the 2,500 shares that were otherwise divided among Eddy, Hammond and Bonner.

The store was up and running, and significantly for its future, C.H. McLeod was the general manager. Herb McLeod was a likeable person and got along easily with people, more so than Hammond, who was often described as shrewd, abrasive and, sometimes, dangerous. Both, however, had an overwhelming desire to improve the Missoula community, although for differing reasons. Hammond's interest leaned more to financial reward, while McLeod seemed to have a genuine interest in participating in and supporting the community and state in which he lived. He was careful, of course, not to offer his support in a way that would be detrimental to the greater Hammond interests. McLeod was the person whom people in Missoula knew, particularly after Hammond left, so how he ran the store and conducted the other aspects of the Mercantile business was what the community saw. In the long run, it would be McLeod's name that would be associated with the Missoula Mercantile Company, not Hammond's.

The boom Missoula Mercantile experienced was, of course, thanks to the two contracts with the Northern Pacific. Unlike other mercantile businesses that relied primarily on credit, MMCo's ability to pay cash and buy wholesale was a distinct advantage. After 1883, when the railroad reached Missoula, it not only enabled the transport of large quantities of goods from both the East and the West but also allowed the store to offer a wide variety of these commodities heretofore unavailable, from stoves to fashionable shades of silk hosiery, such as "crushed strawberry." Ladies' genuine French kid shoes, sealskin caps and elegant silverware were just waiting for the customers to call in. The Missoula Mercantile also bought local products such as flour and apples. More importantly, local farmers could effectively market these products to eastern markets, all due to their tightening relationship with the Northern Pacific. Essentially, the railroad enabled and the expansion of the branch stores allowed stores to buy by the freight carload, which reduced costs dramatically.

Photographs of the store's interior were taken in the 1890s, giving us a general idea of the store's design. As seen on the Sanborn Insurance maps, the bottom floor had seven rooms, each fronting onto Front Street with a door to the street. These long and narrow areas were fairly large, and each held one or more departments: clothing and gentlemen's furnishing goods; dry goods and boots and shoes; hardware, stoves and tinware; groceries; and, on the end, agricultural implements. The furniture department was across Front Street, and so was agricultural implements for a time, while liquor and cigars were housed on the first floor of Hammond's First National Bank.

Furniture department. *No. 80-0057, Archives and Special Collections, Mansfield Library, University of Montana.*

The Missoula Mercantile hardware department. George Beckwith (in rear) would later run the branch store at St. Ignatius. *From the Audrey Kremis Schultz Collection, 2005.062.157b. Used by Permission. All Rights Reserved.*

Buggies were sold across the street from the Missoula Mercantile building. *No. 70-0088, Archives and Special Collections, Mansfield Library, University of Montana.*

The entire store was doing well, and C.H. became more and more enmeshed in Hammond's other various business endeavors. He bought a ranch in Victor, supporting Hammond's development program for the Bitterroot Valley, which was centered in the towns of Victor and Florence. Hammond and McLeod seemed to be working well together. Hammond had informed him in two letters in February 1895 that the Missoula Mercantile could borrow anytime from the First National Bank. "I will see you are not charged a higher rate than can be had here in New York, say 6%," Hammond said. "I believe we are about to enter on an era of great prosperity and our credit and standing 'is gilt edged here' [in New York]." The security of this line of credit would be significant for the future operations of the store. Although Hammond was able to tap New York's financial resources on his own at this point, Bonner was the one who initially opened these doors for E.H. & Company.

But in Missoula, attitudes toward Hammond changed, as his hand appeared to be in everything. In his PhD thesis on Andrew Hammond, Greg

The Missoula Octopus, depicted in Harrison Spaulding's 1890 cartoon. *No. 72-0701 Archives and Special Collections, Mansfield Library, University of Montana.*

Gordon notes that the *Butte Intermountain* referred to the Missoula Mercantile as "an octopus whose slimy tentacles reach out and envelop nearly every farm and ranch and herd and even the forest land of the richest county in the territory." He also mentions that Harrison Spauding, the editor of the *Missoulian*, was so irritated by Hammond's activities that he published a cartoon of Hammond with the head of an octopus, labeling the tentacles with at least twenty-six areas of the greater Missoula community that he felt were controlled by Hammond. Gordon concluded, "Indeed, for many, it seemed that no matter what they did on a daily basis, some portion of each dollar they made flowed into Hammond's pockets." Hammond even controlled the cemetery.

Hammond's immediate response to Spaulding's cartoon was to start his own newspaper to rival the *Missoulian*. He called it the *Missoula Gazette*, and for the next year or so, the two papers went back and forth trading barbs. In the *Gazette*, Hammond explained his philosophy:

> *It is likely that any concern would monopolize the trade of the country if it comes into this county and builds railroads, hotels, sawmills, bank buildings and other buildings of brick and granite blocks and the grandest mercantile establishment in the northwest, while others in the community stand back and howl "monopoly" instead of investing the earnings which have come back to them through the industry and foresight of others. Pluck, perseverance and industry is our motto: nothing more…Let them* [the people] *put their labors in tangible form to save the University of Montana, Fort Missoula, the Flathead Railroad and other contemplated enterprises… We are here to stay and while we are very ready to join with the people in all public enterprises, we are also equally prepared to go it alone.*

This was to be the philosophy by which McLeod would run the Missoula Mercantile, only tempered by a kinder personality. Indeed, Hammond was probably not any more ruthless than his contemporaries Marcus Daly and William Andrew Clark, both known as copper barons. Nevertheless, Hammond's high-handed approach caused resentment, and he and Marcus Daly were often on opposite sides of the fence, though they cooperated on some issues when it suited their financial interests, such as the Montana Improvement Corporation.

Daly took his stand against Hammond in the Bitterroot, where he established the new community of Hamilton to rival Hammond's involvement in Victor and Florence and the Bitterroot Railroad. There, he built a lumber mill and opened his own bank. Nevertheless, Hammond, before he left Missoula in 1894, would offer Daly one-third of the Missoula Mercantile Company stock. This was a portion of the stock that Hammond had purchased from Edward Bonner in 1898 when he bought Bonner out.

Hammond reluctantly offered the rest of Bonner's stock to a wider band of employees in 1904 at the request of C.H. McLeod, who felt he would lose some of his best workers if they were not offered a share in the company. He was correct, and in time, management employees did obtain some of the stock. McLeod explained why he felt it necessary to "coddle" people he worked with in a letter to Hammond dated 1918:

> *We have had to coddle the people of this section ever since I have been connected with the Missoula Mercantile Company. I thought it was necessary to do so in order to develop the business that we have…No doubt this Company would*

Clerks in the retail grocery department. *No. 70-0086, Archives and Special Collections, Mansfield Library, University of Montana.*

> *have been just as successful, or more so, had you remained in Missoula and managed the Missoula Mercantile Company, still if I had undertaken to run this business your way, I would have been ridiculous and unsuccessful, as I cannot see from your viewpoint any more than you can see from mine. By coddling the people tributary to the territory in which we operate, we have built up one of the strongest and most respected business institutions in this commonwealth. You and I aim for the same results, but we have different ways of accomplishing our purposes.*

To understand this new general manager better, the story must return to the Canadian province of New Brunswick. Charles Herbert McLeod was born on February 14, 1859, in Kings County, New Brunswick, Canada. His father was a blacksmith and also maintained a farm. His ancestors were Scottish, from the Isle of Skye, and McLeod often proudly reminded friends and acquaintances of this fact. Formally known as C.H., he was called Herb by his friends. He attended local schools until he was fourteen years old and then left to work on the family farm, an experience that would serve him well. At the age of sixteen, he took a job in the nearby town of Sussex, where he started work as a clerk at McLeod, McKay and Company. He earned $6.50 a month and was earning as much as $400 a year by the time he left. In 1880, the twenty-one-year-old McLeod was offered the job of store clerk by A.B. Hammond at his business in Missoula, Montana, for $1,000 a year. Hammond's name was not unknown to Herb because his cousin, George W. Fenwick, was married to Hammond's sister Mary. Although differing in age by eleven years, Fenwick and McLeod grew up somewhat close to each other in New Brunswick. Mary had suggested Herb to her brother, whom she knew was looking for reliable help for his store in Missoula. George Fenwick, like so many of Hammond's relatives, would follow. He brought his family to Montana by 1885, the year he is recorded as being treasurer of the Big Blackfoot Milling Company in Bonner. He would later be involved in Hammond's Oregon and California lumber businesses.

Herb McLeod came from a big family. He had five brothers—Weldon, William, James, Samuel and Thomas—and two sisters, Lide and Mary. He consistently wrote to his sisters, especially Mary in New Brunswick, which suggests that they were close. In later years, their mother lived with Mary until she died in 1924. Tom followed Herb to Missoula and was made manager of an associated mercantile in Heron along the Northern Pacific line on the Idaho state line in 1885. He also helped Herb with his ranch in the Bitterroot Valley.

Herb McLeod arrived in Missoula on March 29, 1880, to work for E.H. & Company. In 1943, writing a summary of his life, McLeod said, "At that time, I was the only clerk employed, although Mr. Hatheway, who was the bookkeeper, assisted at times in the store when we were busy—which was not very often the case."

Herb became the mainstay of Hammond's enterprises, which was particularly important after Hammond left Missoula in 1894 and moved to Astoria, Oregon, and then to San Francisco, California, where he started the Hammond Lumber Company, another (and bigger) enterprise that later had a shipping company associated with it. Although Hammond's several business ventures are a story in itself, they were often tied to MMCo. It was not uncommon for him to borrow large sums of money from the Missoula Mercantile to help him get through one or more business crises. He did pay back these debts. Occasionally, the MMCo had to postpone purchases or activity because Hammond needed the money.

The key to understanding Hammond's operations is that this connection worked because there was a bond between Hammond and McLeod. This bond grew over the years, McLeod often holding the legal

Photograph of the extended McLeod-Beckwith family, circa 1924. Charles E. Beckwith and his daughter Clara Beckwith McLeod are on the far left and C.H. McLeod is on the far right. *No. 84-0033, Archives and Special Collections, Mansfield Library, University of Montana.*

position of president of a Hammond enterprise while Hammond fronted the financing. But Hammond knew and trusted that McLeod would carry out his wishes. McLeod and Hammond did not always agree but seemed, based on their correspondence, to be able to come to an agreement in those cases. For the most part, Hammond did not offer suggestions on the day-to-day management of the store. And it is useful to remember that they were related, as Clara was C.H.'s wife and Hammond's niece. Hammond's sister Sarah also married Charles Beckwith, who was Clara's father. All of Clara's four sisters' husbands and her two brothers worked for the Mercantile in some capacity during their lives, primarily in management positions.

As McLeod grew older, he would reflect on this relationship, mostly in letters to relatives and close friends:

> *I think I was fortunate* [to have been] *connected with a man of Mr. Hammond's ability and had it not been for his confidence in me, I am afraid I would have continued to be nothing but a clerk; but his faith in me and his*

> *wonderful example stimulated me to accomplish what little I have accomplished during my long years of residence in this state.*

Another letter echoes this sentiment:

> *I was twenty-one years old with very little experience* [and] *did not posses a great deal of ambition, but my association and connection with Mr. Hammond was very fortunate for me. I did not work for him but a short time when he took quite an interest in me and gave me responsibilities, which I think helped me develop more than I would have developed had I been under any other leadership.*
>
> *In 1885*[,] *when the Missoula Mercantile was organized, I was made manager of it at the age of twenty-six and from 1889* [when he became president] *until the present time*[,] *their Montana interests have been under my supervision; and my services seem to please not only Mr. Hammond, but the entire Hammond family which gives me a considerable satisfaction and pleasure.*

McLeod soon became the dominant figure in his own right, but he retained and followed the training he had learned from Hammond for the rest of his life.

Chapter Four

BRANCHING OUT

The Missoula Mercantile's Little Stores

The Northern Pacific contracts for lumber and railroad ties provided E.H. & Company the means to expand its lumber business and its branch stores. These businesses followed the construction crews and brought them not only supplies but also groceries or shoes and a place to spend their paychecks on other sundry items. Frequently set up in a tent, these stores were easy to move when the timber was all cut in an area or the track had been constructed. This is why stores were established in never-heard-of places, like Horse Plains and Weeksville, as rail construction continued west of Missoula. The weekly *Missoulian* in the early 1880s featured a column of news devoted to the happenings in these places. More often than not, the news revolved around E.H. & Company's facilities. Eddy was running this aspect of the business, and the newspaper noted in 1882 that he had sixty men turning out two thousand ties a day for the railroad in the mill at Weeksville. By June, two clerks were working in the Weeksville store. Andrew's brother George, who had initially come west with him, was busy constructing wooden boats to navigate the Clark Fork River between Weeksville and Thompson Falls and move timber more easily.

Nevertheless, these small logging communities were anything but permanent. By 1883, when the railroad was complete, the Weeksville store had moved three miles away to Island City, another community that has since drifted into oblivion. (It might be worth noting that Weeksville was described in the newspaper simply as a "lawless" place where vigilantes had once hanged ten alleged criminals in one day.) The railroad workers were mostly Chinese whose task was to blast rock in order to lay down the steel rails. The loggers in the woods and the sawmill were largely Canadians whom A.B. Hammond had recruited from Quebec and New Brunswick.

Bitterroot Valley Stores

Hammond was not content with working only on the railroad as it expanded westward. Watching the increase of farmers in the Bitterroot Valley south of Missoula, he realized that there would soon be people moving in who would need supplies and crops to ship out. As aforementioned, E.H. & Company purchased Jeremiah Fahey's general merchandising store in Stevensville in 1878. He was a freighter who also had a store at Gibbonsville on the Idaho border. As relayed in this *Missoulian* article, Hammond was continually searching for ways to improve service to keep customers pleased:

> *At present a well-assorted stock is kept on hand, not large of course but up weekly from well-filled warehouses of Eddy Hammond and Co. and sold at Missoula prices. But the next season, the purchases for the house will be made separately and shipped directly to Stevensville in the original packages saving expense in the matter of handling and warranting the customer new and fresh goods.*

There was a robbery at the Stevensville Mercantile in 1885, as reported in the *Stevensville Genesis*, a bicentennial project on the history of Stevensville. The Mercantile was the only store in town with a safe, and many of the citizens stored their valuables there. At the time it was robbed, the safe contained $10,000 in gold dust. Two customers in

Victor Mercantile. *Jeffrey Langton Collection.*

the store borrowed guns from the store and took off after the robbers, gathering several other men along the way to assist. At midnight, they were able to surround the robbers, capture two and kill one and recover the gold. The Mercantile was so grateful that it gave each man in the posse the choice of buckskin gloves or a Stetson hat as a reward. The West was still fairly rough.

Over time, the presence of Andrew Hammond's enterprises would come and go in Stevensville, tied at one point to the May Mercantile, which took over the Stevensville Mercantile in 1914. But that store lost money for May, and it was eventually sold; the Missoula Mercantile did not maintain a presence in Stevensville.

A more profitable venture was the store at Victor, which started from scratch instead of taking over an existing business. In 1887, Hammond joined with Bonner, T.C. Marshall (Hammond's personal attorney), Sterny Blake (a co-locater of Victor's Curlew mine) and others to form the Victor Townsite Company, the purpose of which was to sell lots on four hundred acres to prospective settlers, essentially reinventing the existing townsite of Garfield while ensuring Hammond control over the community.

Hammond built a Missoula Mercantile branch store there, and Harry Keith, brother of Jack Keith and manager of Hammond's First National Bank in Missoula, was brought in as manager. Harry was also from New Brunswick, which was a plus. The store sold everything from clothing to mining equipment. Its success was noted by soon adding a clerk in 1890. Will Cave already worked in the clothing department in Missoula as a clerk and later become known to Missoulians for his history columns in the newspaper.

The success of the store was largely due to Hammond and his cohorts' ability to bring the railroad to Victor. Federal law restricted the Northern Pacific from building branch lines. However, railroads were permitted to buy the line from someone else who had built it. Hammond had tried to build such a line twice before and had been unsuccessful. The third time, he involved Samuel T. Hauser, the Helena banker and recent territorial governor, who had already invested in Victor's Curlew Mine.

The Missoula and Bitter Root Valley Railroad Company was, not surprisingly, soon purchased by the Northern Pacific, and transportation to and from the Bitterroot Valley blossomed. There had been a question of which side of the Bitterroot River to build the track on. Hauser's mine was on the east side, but Victor historian Jeffrey Langton relates that it was Hammond who decided that the railroad should go through Victor on the west side, allowing Victor to become a rail center rather than the already established Stevensville, which was on the east side of the river. He also had hopes of making Victor the county seat, but that hope was eventually squashed by Marcus Daly, who established his town of Hamilton farther south. Today's Highway 93 follows the railway's route, and cars pass speedily through Victor on their way to Hamilton from Missoula. The railway carried passengers for the first time in December 1887. Among the thirty-five dignitaries were Hammond, Bonner, Eddy, Hauser and the governor, Preston Leslie. Hammond then hosted a fancy dinner for them in Missoula, concluding with coffee and cognac.

Victor did become a center, although its heyday is now long past. By 1909, it had a 100,000-bushel grain elevator, a livestock yard and two fifty-car capacity warehouses along the Northern Pacific tracks. All except the livestock yard were related to the MMCo. Harking back to A.B.'s own ranching experience, the store would wisely extend credit until the end of the season, knowing the cash for farmers was often hard to obtain before harvest time. The store, however, was not shy about taking a mortgage on a farmer's property or even foreclosing. Several of the early ads for the store promoted ranches for sale, likely acquired in this manner.

Hammond also opened a store in Corvallis in 1889, just south of Stevensville and northeast of Hamilton. Although initially prosperous, it did not succeed and was closed by 1898, hindered by the presence of rival Marcus Daly, who had staked out Hamilton and the surrounding area as his domain.

Flathead Reservation Stores

Hammond was not neglectful of the expanding opportunities to the north as well and was certainly not thwarted by the fact that most of land was already part of the Flathead Indian Reservation. He, through, the efforts of C.H. McLeod, pushed hard for the opening of the reservation to white settlers, which eventually occurred in 1910.

In 1881, E.H. & Company purchased the stores of T.J. Demers in Frenchtown, just west of Missoula. Demers was a well-known trader, said to be a "big man in this part of the country as well as having an unlimited credit with business firms in the East," according to an early history of Frenchtown. Hammond immediately closed the Frenchtown store, as it was far from the railroad, and moved the Frenchtown merchandise to the Missoula store.

Hammond also bought Demers's store at the Flathead Indian Agency at Jocko, although Demers operated that store until November 1882. Hammond soon had three men working there. In the summer of 1883, he moved the Jocko store four miles to Arlee to be on the rail line. The Arlee store continued in the Missoula Mercantile family into the 1960s, and Walter McLeod, C.H.'s son, became its president in 1942.

Hammond also bought partial interest in the store at St. Ignatius on the reservation, the site of the Jesuit mission and later its school. The store was run by a relative of T.J.'s named Alex Demers. In 1902, Alex sold his interests to George Beckwith, who was C.H. McLeod's brother-in-law and also from New Brunswick. Beckwith arrived in 1886 and was soon working for MMCo in Missoula. George then ran the store with his two sons. In 1907, George Beckwith was making a profit in his store of $5,000 as reported by C.H. McLeod, so it was considered a viable business.

Beckwith Mercantile in St. Ignatius. *No. 84-0035, Archives and Special Collections, Mansfield Library, University of Montana.*

Beckwith's son, Jack, recounted some memories of the store in an oral interview:

> *I had had enough bookkeeping in high school that I took over the bookkeeping for my father. My brother worked in the store. We handled everything from thrashing machines to ladies' brassieres… We had grain elevators in St. Ignatius and another one down in Ravalli where the railhead was. Father bought a five-ton Pierce-Arrow truck that he used to haul the grain down from St. Ignatius to Ravalli in, with hard rubber tires on it.*
>
> *In the store that my father had, the Indians came in to trade, and very few of them could speak any English at all. But they all trusted my father. They all had cattle. There was no bank there and they would bring their money to my father. He would keep track of it in a conventional way, but he gave them something, some* [estimate] *of how much they had. He started giving them nails. A nail* [60d] *was worth sixty dollars and a* [40d] *nail was forty dollars and so on down. Of course, the Indians could come in and buy all the nails they wanted. He had*

> *many thousands of dollars that they trusted him with. The only thing they had as evidence was the nails. But he never once had an Indian try to run an extra nail in on him. They were always honest.*

MMCo's connections with what came to be called the Beckwith Mercantile lasted into the 1960s. George became the first mayor of St. Ignatius in 1938, and his sons ran the store after his death, changing the name to Beckwith Brothers.

A brother of George's, Andrew Beckwith, ran the Hot Springs Commercial Company, also on the reservation, for the Mercantile in the 1920s. He seems to have had more difficulty in making ends meet, and C.H. McLeod was constantly reminding him to not give so much credit and to reduce surplus stock. Still, McLeod was philosophical: "We have to have a reasonable assortment of merchandise in order to do a profitable business, because we cannot sell enough goods at Hot Springs to make even a stand-off unless we have a reasonable stock."

Kalispell: The Big Branch Store

What would eventually become the largest mercantile in the Flathead valley region began as a mercantile store in the town of Demersville, named for T.J. Demers, the store's owner. *Flathead Facts*, a booklet about Missoula County published in 1890, described it as a "monster tent." After Demers died in 1888, the Missoula Mercantile acquired the property. As the booklet describes, a "substantial building was erected 30 X 60' with a warehouse attached of similar size. Ice houses, stables and offices were in the rear." It goes on to describe the store's relation with the Mercantile in Missoula: "Now belonging to and manipulated by the Missoula Mercantile, is the largest and best-known business house in the Flathead section."

Harry Keith, the manager of the Victor Mercantile, was selected to be the new manager at Demersville. The town itself was located on the Flathead River, several navigable miles upriver from Flathead Lake and southeast of the present city of Kalispell. Similar to the situation with the Northern Pacific, several towns vied for the financial honor of being the division point (where railroad offices and trains would be stored) for the Great Northern Railway that was then being constructed from St. Paul to Seattle. Its progress already had been a boom for Demersville as the supplies for the railroad construction were shipped from Missoula on the train to Ravalli; they were then transferred by boat to the bottom of Flathead Lake and then by steamboat to Demersville, where it was said as many as one hundred teams of horses a day unloaded the cargo and took it to the construction sites. As it turned out, none of the towns was successful. The railroad chose an entirely new location instead for its division point, which would be called Kalispell. Within a day or two, at least half of the town of Demersville, then having some 1,500 people, allegedly moved to the new location; some even moved their buildings.

The Demersville store did not, however, move immediately; in fact, as the story goes, one of the three employees, Lew Switzer, the hardware manager, was ordered to pack up the inventory and send it back to the Mercantile in Missoula. Instead, Switzer traveled to Missoula and somehow convinced C.H. McLeod to move the store to Kalispell. Switzer continued in the new store as buyer for the hardware department until 1907, the year he left to start his own furniture store.

The first site of the Demers Mercantile in Kalispell would not be its last, and by 1897, it had grown substantially and moved to 200 First Avenue East. By then, it employed more than twenty men. This new store was a fifty- by eighty-foot building, with two long bays, one for hardware and one for farm implements. In 1898, a forty-thousand-bushel grain elevator was added. Kalispell, like the Missoula Mercantile, had a delivery service but actually raised Percheron horses to use with its delivery wagons. In 1901, a grocery store was also added, and in 1903, an additional fifty feet was tacked onto the First Avenue side. Similar to the Missoula store, it soon had more than five warehouses along the railroad tracks, in this case, the Great Northern. In 1911, the store, which now looked rather like the Missoula store, was renamed the Kalispell Mercantile, with Harry Keith as vice-president and general manager and C.H. McLeod as president. This firm's territory ran from Havre in eastern Montana to Bonners Ferry, Edward Bonner's old stomping ground, on the west. It extended ninety miles northwest toward the Canadian border.

Harry Keith remained general manager until his death in 1932. By 1926, the store had eighty-five full-time employees and was booming. A devastating fire destroyed the grain elevator in 1945, but later expansions to

Harry Keith (in the foreground, to the right) in the Kalispell Mercantile office. *No. 001-viii_78_16_186, Archives and Special Collections, Mansfield Library, University of Montana.*

Kalispell Mercantile warehouse. *No. 76-0100, Archives and Special Collections, Mansfield Library, University of Montana.*

Kalispell Mercantile. *No. 78-0306, Archives and Special Collections, Mansfield Library, University of Montana.*

the store allowed the Kalispell Mercantile to remain a dynamic element in the Missoula Mercantile system, long after the Missoula store was bought out and renamed the Montana Mercantile. Katheryn McKay, in her book on historic Kalispell, noted that current owners of the building have removed a 1960s façade from the second floor, "thus returning this important business block to its former glory."

Bonner: The Company Store

A slightly different store was set up in the town of Bonner, just east of Missoula, where Hammond, through the Montana Improvement Company, had built his permanent sawmill in 1887. He had also built a town there with neat houses for the management staff, as well as a company store where the workers and their families, who lived in adjacent neighborhoods, could buy on credit. The amounts were usually deducted from their wages. Hammond also built The Margaret, a huge Victorian hotel that stood adjacent to the mill until the Anaconda Company tore it down in 1957. It was used for guests, although some millworkers also

Hammond's Bonner Sawmill built in 1887. *No. 78-0371 186, Archives and Special Collections, Mansfield Library, University of Montana.*

lived there. Hotel registers remain that show that Hammond, McLeod, Daly and other dignitaries visited in the late 1800s.

Anything the employees of the mill wanted but could not buy at the company store could be shipped from the Missoula Mercantile. The prices were the same as at the store in Missoula, following the system Hammond had set up in Stevensville many years before. Interestingly, this system continued long after Hammond interests no longer owned the mill, having been acquired by Marcus Daly in 1898. The mill was subsequently owned by his company, the Anaconda Copper Mining Company, and it became the largest sawmill between Minneapolis and the West Coast.

Lois Johnson, who grew up in Bonner, remembered how excited she was when her parents bought a twenty-dollar coupon at the store for her and her siblings to spend at the Missoula Mercantile. The Bonner community was connected to Missoula by the electric streetcar. The "Bonner Bench" sat in front of the MMCo on Front Street and was put there by C.H. so that Bonner customers could wait for the streetcar.

Later, after the streetcar's demise, it served as a bus stop. Anaconda discontinued the store in 1945.

A Look Inside a Branch Store

A description of the store layout from the *Story of Bonner, Montana: A Grassroots Tribute* is quoted here because there is no such extant description of the Missoula store. Although this store might have been larger than the branch stores at Victor or Beckwith Mercantile at St. Ignatius, its layout would have been similar.

> *Mostly canned and bottled groceries were displayed on the shelves on one side of the store and dry goods and notions and sewing material on the other side. On the front end of the store on one side was a glass enclosed display case in which were kept a small but adequate supply of patent medicines and miscellaneous home health, and dental care products. On the counter near the front door was a glass enclosed display case for packaged and bulk candy and gum. Another glass case held tobacco, including chewing tobacco and snuff used by quite a few of the mill workers and lumberjacks.*
>
> *Tables in the rear portion of the store displayed an assortment of work clothing and shoes for the mill workers and ranchers to buy. Dress shoes were also sold there. Under the counter and grocery display shelves were enclosed wooden bins from which the clerks could scoop into sacks small quantities of sugar, flour, beans, etc. for customers who wanted to carry home some of their groceries. Large sacks of these products were delivered to customers' homes. In bins and on shelves in the back of the store was kept a good supply of nails and some small hardware items, also household paints and brushes, and cleaning equipment like shovels and brooms.*
>
> *A large warehouse with* [a] *full basement was attached to the rear section of the store building in which to stock large quantities of canned goods and potatoes and carrots hauled in from farms for the customers' needs…*
>
> *There was no self-service in this store. There were enough clerks on hand at all times to serve the customers across the counters. In addition, several times a week a clerk went out to customers' homes in the surrounding communities to solicit their needs for groceries…*

Most every customer had a charge account at the store. Employees at the Bonner mill could also arrange to have their grocery bills "taken out" of their wages each month or pay period, as the Lumber Department bookkeeper also kept the accounts for the store. Employees of the mill, and store customers, could also get a "purchase order" from the store manager, with which to purchase goods at the Missoula Mercantile that were not carried in stock at the Bonner Store and have the charge handled through the payroll.

Chapter Five

McLEOD'S STORE

Hammond's Legacy

Since Hammond's departure from Missoula in 1894, C.H. McLeod was ostensibly fully in charge of the Missoula Mercantile and all of its branch stores. However, until his death in 1934, Hammond would remain a strong figure in McLeod's life and would correspond with him regularly, no doubt because the financial success of the Missoula Mercantile was so important to the success of Hammond's other enterprises.

However, even before Hammond left Missoula, he had begun to divest himself of some of these enterprises, looking to invest the money and time in new opportunities in Oregon and then California. By 1913, Hammond had written to McLeod, telling him, "I am in favor of selling all our real estate in Missoula as fast as we have an opportunity." That included the Missoula Mercantile. Hammond continued:

> *I am willing, however, to stay with you as long as you care to assume the responsibility. I believe that it will always be a great responsibility and one that you will have to stay with constantly for up to this time you have not been able to develop anybody in the business outside of yourself, who even thinks they could run it in case you should desire to leave Missoula.*

Corner of Gerald and University Avenues in Missoula with Hammond Avenue filled in.
Author's collection.

McLeod responded:

> *It has been the moral obligation that I felt was due you which has kept me here, doing the best I have been able to do, but if any plan can be thought of whereby we could dispose of our mercantile interests in Western Montana, it would be more than agreeable to me…The country is so small that if a business as large as ours is prosperous, every other dealer must go broke or struggle along without making money…They do not blame themselves for lack of ability or capital, but think they are injured by the unfair methods of their strong competitors*

McLeod essentially reasoned that they could not dispose of the business, and while he might not have been able to ignore Hammond, it seemed people in Missoula gradually began to forget about Hammond and their disgruntlement over his octopus-like hands in Missoula's economy. Indeed, there is little physical evidence in the community to remind us today of the vast influence that Hammond had over Missoula. There are no statues or plaques that honor this man, nor are there any streets or parks named after him (although his wife has a street named after her). In the University District, one street was originally called Hammond Avenue, but the Higgins family, continuing the old rivalry, succeeded in having it renamed after one of C.P. Higgins's children, Gerald, after Hammond left Missoula. Interestingly, Hammond Avenue is still stamped on the sidewalk, on the one corner of Gerald and University, although partially eradicated on another. Even his Four Corners have changed.

The Four Corners

Hammond once owned all the four corners of Higgins and Front (formerly Mullan Road) in the center of downtown Missoula. Each corner was marked with his large, imposing buildings: the Missoula Mercantile, the First National Bank, the Hammond Building and the Florence Hotel. In the 1930s, two of these edifices burned and were then rebuilt, neither in the style of the original building.

Hammond had wrested control of the First National Bank from C.P. Higgins in 1889 and become its president. Hammond erected a very imposing granite and brick building with a turret for the bank. He used the bank's power freely, often for the benefit of Missoula; for example, he prevented a run on the First National Bank when the Panic of 1893 hit Missoula by calling on funds from the Missoula Mercantile Company and others. The panic caused runs on the other Missoula banks, including Higgins's Western Montana National Bank, and Hammond realized that to lose them all would have brought financial disaster to Missoula.

Although Hammond sold his interests in the bank to A.F. Lusk in 1909, his building remained until it was torn down in 1962 and replaced by a more modern version, which was also torn down and replaced in 2009 by a taller and more energy-efficient building. Still housing the bank, it is now called the First Interstate Bank, and it claims to be the oldest continuously operating bank in the state.

Northern Pacific Railroad map of Missoula in 1891 featuring Hammond buildings. *Library of Congress.*

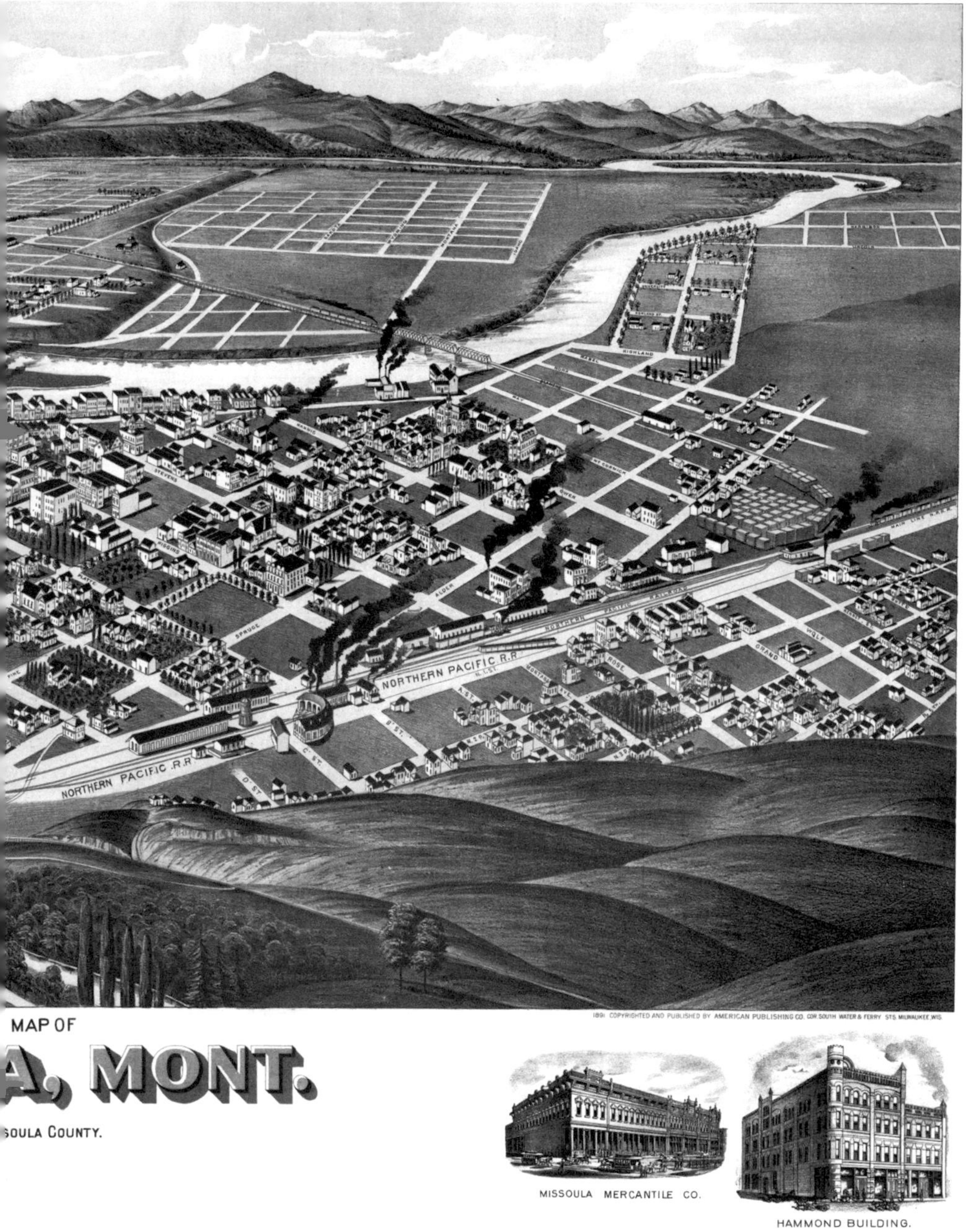

1891 COPYRIGHTED AND PUBLISHED BY AMERICAN PUBLISHING CO. COR. SOUTH WATER & FERRY STS. MILWAUKEE, WIS.

MAP OF

A, MONT.

SOULA COUNTY.

MISSOULA MERCANTILE CO.

HAMMOND BUILDING.

Another dominating four-story stone Hammond building, also with a turret, was once located diagonally across the street from the Mercantile until it burned in 1932. Three floors were used by Montana Power Company, and Hammond's offices were on the top floor. Using the insurance money, it was rebuilt in 1933 by the Hammond Building Company (yet another Hammond operation), although in a much-reduced form. Butte architect R.C. Hugenin is credited with its Art Deco design, and the building is known today as the Hammond Arcade, now something of an overlooked commercial space. Interestingly, even though finances required its rebuilding be reduced from two stories to one, it was one of the few large commercial buildings constructed in the city during the Depression and, therefore, was a help to Missoula's struggling economy. It is now listed on the National Register of Historic Places. The Missoula Drug Company, one of the tenants in the original Hammond Building, resurfaced in the new Hammond Arcade. However, Montana Power Company went elsewhere in Missoula. Hammond's own offices were no longer needed since he had died and had been used only on occasion after he left Missoula.

The Florence Hotel burned in 1913, and although it was rebuilt, it burned again in 1936. Only through the efforts of C.H. McLeod and his son Walter was it rebuilt a second time. Although Hammond had tried unsuccessfully to sell the hotel, the building still stands today and currently houses offices and a restaurant. It remained a hotel until 1973, when it was sold and became the Glacier Building. A more recent owner, ALPS, undertook a major restoration of the interior and, in 1996, received the Missoula Historic Preservation Award for Excellence in the area of Compatible Addition to a Historic Structure. The entrance lobby, restored to elegance, looks like it did when the hotel was at its heyday. In early 2012, potential new owners have suggested they would like to return it to hotel status within five years and make it a five-star hotel.

The Missoula Mercantile building still occupies the fourth corner, and today, the store is poised to enter a new era, even though it will not be as a department store. It was listed in the National Register of Historic Places in 1990. Its new owners, Octagon Partners, are planning the historic restoration of the building as the backdrop for new uses and are, at the time of this writing, in the midst of obtaining necessary approvals from the State Historic Preservation Commission and the National Park Service that administers the National Historic Register on which the building is listed. The new Missoula Mercantile is slated to include offices and restaurants, maintaining the historic footprint of the old business and preserving the lynchpin of downtown Missoula.

C.H. McLeod Takes Over

Instead of A.B. Hammond, it is Charles Herbert McLeod who is commemorated on these four corners and elsewhere in Missoula. A large brass plaque commemorating him as an "inspiration to the community" and his "generous contributions" to the development of Missoula hangs in the entrance hallway of the Florence and was placed there after McLeod's death in 1946. It charts the rebuilding of the hotel as a "monument to his vision and his faith in Missoula."

McLeod ran a tight ship but seemed to be well liked by his employees. He was seen as generous and always had his door open, but he could be tough in his decisions that affected the future of Missoula and the Missoula Mercantile. According to a bicentennial history of Missoula in the July 2, 1976 *Missoulian*, in 1917, the Great Western Sugar Company built a plant in Missoula and planned to market itself through the Missoula Mercantile and its branches, but when the company was unable to agree on terms with McLeod, it sold out and, in 1922, was replaced by the more agreeable Amalgamated Sugar Company. In *Red Ribbons*, John Toole relates that during the Depression, McLeod, a staunch Republican, led a group of Missoula businessmen to remind the mayor and city council that instead of getting

Plaque dedicated to Charles H. McLeod in the Florence Hotel, 1946. *No. 002-XXVI_007, Archives and Special Collections, Mansfield Library, University of Montana.*

on a moral high horse about Roosevelt's government assistance programs, they should be seeking all the federal aid they could in order to keep up with Great Falls, which had a new civic center, and Billings, where a new city hall had just been constructed.

McLeod gave very generous terms to farmers during the Depression so that they would not go under. The Missoula Mercantile loaned money to many who could not get loans from the bank. It always kept a hefty amount in the vault on the second floor and could always meet payroll, even when Roosevelt closed the banks in 1933. Jim Meyers, who would become general manager of the store, remembered the days when C.H. was in charge. "He would get nervous when the bank balance would get below $500,000," said Meyers. "He'd call New York Guaranteed Trust and borrow $100,000."

McLeod's management style was what might today be described as "micro-management": he seemed to be involved in every aspect and detail of the store. One former employee said, "Nothing happened without his approval." Although each department head was responsible for his department, McLeod kept sharp track of what was going on. One story was told about an employee whom McLeod had fired, and McLeod had been rather surprised to see him in the store at his job the following week. When McLeod inquired why, the man replied, "Yes, indeed, he had been fired, but he needed the Missoula Mercantile more than the Mercantile needed him gone." The man proved to be an exemplary employee for the next thirty years.

Much of what we know about McLeod comes from his extensive correspondence. The large number of issues McLeod dealt with on any one day is significant, and he proved to be knowledgeable and up-to-date on issues. He wrote almost daily to Hammond to keep him updated on the many enterprises in which the Missoula Mercantile was financially involved.

In early 1900, C.H. wrote to the Big Blackfoot Milling Company, as he was interested to learn how many apple boxes the company sold to Bitterroot orchardists. In his letters, he said he was "assisting" the Northern Pacific in obtaining a better freight rate for apples to eastern markets, which of course would be sold through the Missoula Mercantile. In another, he tried to orchestrate the redistribution of stock of the Eddy Hammond & Company of Delaware to allow shares of stock in the Missoula Mercantile to be owned by at least some of his long-term employees. This required letters to all the stockholders, including the widow of Marcus Daly, as well as convincing Hammond, who was always leery of letting many into the inner circle of shareholders.

Glassware department. *Pictorial Histories Publishing Company.*

Some of the letters dealt specifically with the store, such as one that discussed the welfare of a night watchman who had twice become intoxicated on the job yet needed wages to live on, or another that proposed an expansion of the store to Hammond. In others, McLeod wrote about the community or Hammond-related enterprises. In one letter, he commented favorably on the new streetcar line in Missoula; in another, he discussed selling properties from Hammond's Missoula Real Estate Association. He explored U.S. senator William Clark's proposed dam downstream from the Bonner Mill and its possible effects. He wrote letters supporting legislation for the opening of the Flathead Indian Reservation to white settlers (where the Mercantile already had a presence but wanted more) and letters that described the expansion of Fort Missoula, which could lead to more government contracts for Missoula. He even had time to send a note to the Catholic Ladies Group of Plains, promising to chair at its upcoming fair. It is little wonder that he was not able to find anyone else to be as knowledgeably engaged as him on all these issues to assume his job.

Hardware department. *Pictorial Histories Publishing Company.*

McLeod's correspondence generally included a paragraph of how business was going. In a letter to his sister Mary, dated November 1936, he wrote:

> *For the last two months our business at Missoula has gone over the $500,000 a month mark, and if our business was as good every month…it would mean $6,000,000 a year, which is a great increase from the time I went to work for the company—at that time we were doing a business of about $125,000 a year.*

Much of his time was spent responding to requests from A.B. Hammond, who frequently asked McLeod to act as his political emissary. For example, in 1909, Hammond wrote, "Can you arrange to have some of the lumbermen in Missoula write to Senators [Tom] Carter and [Joseph] Dixon (the Montana U.S. senators) asking them to do what they can to prevent a reduction in the tariff on lumber?" A month later, after giving McLeod approval to sell half a block of land from the company's holding on the south side of Missoula to the same Senator Dixon, Hammond explained, "Joe is a good fellow and we wish to encourage him and every other good man who has a family to build a good home on the south side [of Missoula]." Later, in 1922, when Dixon was governor and tried to decline speaking at

One of many Mercantile warehouses around Missoula. *Pictorial Histories Publishing Company.*

the District Convention of Rotary Clubs in Missoula, McLeod wired him in no uncertain terms: "You will have to reverse your decision…You must come even if the urgent business affairs of the state have to be suspended for a short time." Dixon came.

By the late 1920s, the Missoula Mercantile had a full-time attorney on staff. "George Shepard still spends most of his time with the politicians," McLeod wrote, "trying to get things done for Western Montana, which will be beneficial to all of us in this section." R.H. "Ty" Robinson, who was Shepard's successor as the Mercantile's attorney, noted that Shepard had an unlimited expense account to accomplish his task, something that Ty did not inherit with the job.

Hammond, in 1910, suggested that McLeod come to the West Coast and spend more time with Hammond Lumber interests, but he realized that McLeod might be too busy juggling the Missoula interests to take on any more tasks. McLeod, for his part, did not jump at the chance and never appeared to seriously consider moving to the coast (though it comes up more than once in their correspondence).

Hammond, operating from California, remained in the background but was still in charge of many of the issues: in a letter to John Keith (treasurer of the First National Bank), in 1909, Hammond wrote that he wanted

Art Nouveau–style door at the Mercantile's front entrance, part of the store's remodel by C.H. McLeod, circa 1915. *No. 001-VIII_78-08_109, Archives and Special Collections, Mansfield Library, University of Montana.*

a meeting held whereby McLeod was not only made a director of the Missoula Real Estate Association but also made president of it, explaining simply that as McLeod had "control of the real estate properties as well as the Missoula Mercantile, he should be president of these Companies." Hammond wrote a similar letter in regards to the South Missoula Land Company, the second of Hammond's real estate companies in Missoula. Also in 1909, Hammond wrote to McLeod that he had received a bank statement that documented that the First National Bank had over $1 million in cash on hand. "You had better deposit the surplus funds of the two real estate companies with the Hammond Lumber Company. We can use it and pay you interest." Here is the true value of the Missoula Mercantile to Hammond's enterprises.

Chapter Six

WORKING AT THE MISSOULA MERCANTILE

It was generally acknowledged that the employees of the Missoula Mercantile did not receive high salaries. There wasn't a health insurance plan, and the retirement plan was not actually a plan. What made these employees so loyal to the Missoula Mercantile then? What follows is a brief account of some of the working conditions over time at the Missoula Mercantile.

Perks, Pensions and Payday

In many ways, working at the Missoula Mercantile was like having a large family. Even though employees did not receive health insurance, if someone got sick, that person was taken care of. In case after case, employees' medical expenses were paid off, and their jobs were held while they recovered. In a letter to a potential employee in 1920, Walter McLeod explained: "We have an insurance plan here whereby our employees' wages are secured in case of sickness, a very small cost, which has proven very satisfactory to all of our people."

The Missoula Mercantile plumbing department, circa 1906. *The Macy's Collection, 2005.003.65. Used by Permission. All Rights Reserved.*

Many times when they were out of the office, the secretaries would report in letters to both C.H and Walter if one of the employees fell ill and that they (the secretaries) had visited during lunch or read the newspaper to them. Such an act was not perceived as a job, just a kindness to a fellow employee.

There were some perks working for the Mercantile. Gordon Swanson, who began part-time work at the Missoula Mercantile in 1938 while in high school, recounts that after working ninety days, employees got a 10 percent discount, which increased to 15 percent. Swanson later got a 20 to 25 percent discount as a manager. Employees in 1913 were requested to do personal shopping before 10:30 a.m. and to avoid shopping on

The millinery department, late 1890s. *No. 94-3155, Archives and Special Collections, Mansfield Library, University of Montana.*

Saturdays. This seems to have been a much-discussed subject, and a later employee manual sets the hours earlier and prohibits employees from shopping at all on Saturdays. In general, the employees did receive a Christmas bonus.

There was not a pension plan, although before Social Security was established in 1935, small bonuses were given to long-term employees when they retired. After 1935, the Mercantile would make up the difference between Social Security and $300 when an employee retired, but the wording of its policy was such that it only applied as long as the Missoula Mercantile was able to pay it. By 1948, there were still thirteen employees who had worked forty years or more and another sixteen who had worked thirty or more years. C.H.'s son, Walter McLeod, was in that group, as he had started in 1911. Another twenty-nine employees had worked twenty or more years.

Establishing a pension plan would become a challenge to Walter when he was in charge as manager, and there was still not a pension plan when the store downsized in the 1950s. Walter had the uncomfortable job of writing to long-term employees and telling them that the contribution that the Missoula Mercantile had been making to them for their retirement would end on January 1, 1960. "Now that the Missoula Mercantile has been sold, we do not have the income to support the constantly growing program." He noted that they had tried to establish a pension fund in the 1940s but did not have the means to do it for all. The reason, as he explained to Florence Hammond, Andrew's daughter and a stockholder, was that "we cannot do everything and still pay the stockholders a dividend."

How the employees were paid over the years is interesting. The 1913 manual states that "salaries will be paid at six o'clock on Wednesday evening or on Thursday up to 10:30 a.m. Employees are requested to call for their envelopes between those hours." Hope Stockstad, a bookkeeper who worked at the Missoula Mercantile in the 1950s, described a remarkably similar circumstance. The accounting department had to have payroll calculated by 3:00 p.m. on Wednesday, and then two of the "bosses" would go over to the First National Bank across the street and bring the payroll back in a leather pouch. She and another woman would then count it out into the small brown envelopes for the employees who would pick it up. She indicated that the managers were paid by check at that time.

Veterans

World War I and World War II took their toll on the employees remaining at the store. During World War I, C.H. held regular "jolly-ups" for the employees to get them together and to honor the "sixteen Missoula Mercantile boys who are representing the 'Reliable old Store' at the front." A flag was unfurled, and employees sang "The Star-Spangled Banner" and danced until the early hours of the morning. C.H. encouraged the boys to write to him and told them their jobs would be waiting for them when they returned, no doubt comforting thoughts for those who were so far away from home.

During World War II, there were seventeen employees who left their jobs to serve, plus an additional twenty-five new employees who served in the war. As in the previous war, the jobs of those who served were kept open for when they returned. Gordon Swanson returned in 1946 to work full time in the shoe department. Moreover, C.H. sent him to the university to improve

Shoe department, early 1900s. *No. 001-VIII_78-11_149, Archives and Special Collections, Mansfield Library, University of Montana.*

his math and business skills, and he subsequently advanced to department manager and retired in 1959 as department sales manager for the Allied Department Store Company after it acquired the Missoula Mercantile (the store was then known as the Bon), spending a total of forty-three years with the Mercantile. Even then, his skills were still in demand, and he was called back to help manage the Missoula store, which he agreed to do at twenty hours a week. He finally retired (officially) in 1992.

Dealing with Customers

The 1913 *Instructions for the Guidance of Employees* gives employees firm reminders as to how they should handle customers in the store: "No matter how foolish the customer's complaint may be, remember it is a serious matter with the customer."

Some form of this document existed though the 1950s, and it continued to be updated.

It was not until after the 1959 merger of the store with Allied Department Stores that specialized pamphlets appeared, such as the thirty-two-page booklet *System Training Manual for Salespeople*, which describes how salespersons were to ring up sales as cash or charge, deliver a package and deal with layaway and in-store discounts.

Loyalty to the Store

Since the store's beginning, employees found that loyalty to "our store" was implicitly required. The 1913 employee manual stressed, "Be unwavering in your loyalty to 'Our Store.'"

In fact, longevity and loyalty were the words most often applied to employees. C.H. worked for sixty-six years. His secretary, Amelia Loffness, began working for the firm when she was eighteen and was his secretary for over forty years until he retired. She would ultimately work for the Missoula Mercantile for fifty-three years. After C.H. retired, she continued to type his letters, often keeping him company at dinner (his wife had died in 1935 and he lived alone) and reading the newspaper to him after his sight failed.

In 1943, a testimonial dinner was given in honor of Mrs. Kate Hoon, who was retiring after 34 years of service to the Missoula Mercantile in the ladies' ready-to-wear department. The *Missoulian* reported that eighty-five employees representing 1,920 years of service were present, surely an impressive number.

O.C. Garlington, the freight traffic manager, had started out working for the Northern Pacific Railroad in its freight office before transferring to the Missoula Mercantile in 1908. He became the expert on freight rates and practices, which was essential for a firm that was becoming increasingly dependent on moving goods around the country as most of its business was in wholesale. As Jim Meyers related in his oral history, "The Northern Pacific people would check with him [Garlington] on certain things because he knew what the tariffs were and what the rates were better than some of the people that worked over at the Northern Pacific. He had forty-two years of continuous service with the Missoula Mercantile."

The office of the Missoula Mercantile. O.C. Garlington is sitting at his desk on the left, and George McAllister is in the back. On the right are Harry Canwart, John J. Inch and John Mahoney. *The Macy's Collection, 2010.003.074. Used by Permission. All Rights Reserved.*

George B. Wilcox, who retired in 1950 at the same time as Garlington, was a hardware department employee for over fifty years, starting out as a clerk and ending up as a buyer. During that time, the number of hardware employees increased from nine to over sixty, and the number of departments increased from nine to twenty-three.

Ray G. Bailey retired at age seventy-four in 1959 as manager of the dry goods and women's accessories departments and had been with the firm since 1908, working as a manager for all but three of his fifty-one years as a Mercantile employee. He bought regularly in Chicago and New York for the store, explaining his philosophy as "quality over price," believing that "quality keeps the customer coming back." He noted that the Missoula Mercantile, the largest store in Montana at that time, had a volume among the highest in the country relative to population because of the firm's "policy of putting customer satisfaction ahead of concern with sales figures."

J.M. Busey, manager of the Missoula Mercantile's wholesale grocery department, retired in 1949 after working for the company for forty-eight years. He worked in Kalispell for twenty years and then in Missoula for an additional twenty-eight. He also organized and helped establish the wholesale drug and cold storage and locker departments in the warehouse adjacent to the Northern Pacific lines in Missoula and was a member of the board of directors of the Kalispell Mercantile (a separate but related corporation to the Missoula Mercantile). Significantly, he helped initiate a voluntary association of western Montana grocery stores that became known as Red and White Grocery Stores, which the Missoula Mercantile was the major player of, until the company realized that it was undercutting its own retail grocery department, which it then closed.

Unions or Not

One aspect of employee life not yet mentioned was employees' relationship with unions. Both Hammond and McLeod were dead set against having the store employees unionized. From their perspective, there wasn't a positive return from unions but many potential detrimental aspects. In a 1945 letter to his granddaughter Clara Marsh, C.H. expounded on this:

> *During my many years in management, we were never unionized and I never had a committee of our employees wait upon me with a grievance, nor did we have unpleasantness of any kind within our organization. The same condition exists today under your father's management. My opinion is that when employees become unionized* [here, he references the fact that there are only 250 to 300 workers at the Mercantile], *they think more of their unions than they do of their employers.*

There had been a few attempts to unionize. In 1914, McLeod wrote to Hammond in California, telling him that there had been an effort to get the Mercantile employees to join the Clerks Union and that deliverymen had told McLeod that if McLeod did not, the union would boycott the store. McLeod took no such steps but told Hammond, "They have a man carrying a banner in front of our store declaring us 'unfair,' and every delivery man working for other concerns is doing all he can to injure our business around town."

Although it affected restaurants and small businesses in town, it had, he noted, not affected the Missoula Mercantile's out-of-town business. McLeod's strategy was to let the strike continue, predicting it would die off on its own due to the effect on the small shopkeepers. He felt the Mercantile Company was big enough to withstand a short period of Missoula customers not buying at the store. The employees had not expressed an interest in joining.

The store was also picketed when the Industrial Workers of the World (IWW, or Wobblies) activity started up against the Bonner Mill in the early 1900s. The picketing was not a result of the store's involvement with the mill but because the Mercantile Company was the largest employer in the county. It was winter, and C.H.'s response was to empty out the coat department and give coats to the strikers to keep them from freezing as they marched up and down.

An internal organization called the Missoula Mercantile Company Employees Protective Association was formed in 1919. It was an attempt by the company to forestall unionization, and it lasted through 1948.

In the 1960s, there was a strike against the wholesale grocery department, which was located in the large warehouse by the Northern Pacific tracks. Jim Meyers, the store manager at the time, thought it was unfair that they picketed the retail store and noted in his oral history that the strike went on a year and a day, explaining that Missoula Mercantile was now operating under the Allied Department Store and that Allied had a labor attorney who flew over from Seattle regularly to advise. There was eventually a vote, and the employees voted two to one against the union.

Buyers for the Mercantile

At the beginning, it was Hammond and Bonner who did the buying in San Francisco and Helena, but by the 1890s, the Missoula Mercantile had buyers who made trips to New York several times a year to buy next season's clothes.

In 1895, Hammond arranged free transportation for these buyers on the Pennsylvania Railroad.

Miss Kate Doughty was the buyer for women's clothing in 1922, and it was Walter McLeod who kept her abreast of her department while she was away, occasionally advising her of a client's special request. The Mercantile prided itself on knowing its customers. "Mrs. K, wants a white suit, not serge or fancy, but [it] has to fit tight and be more or less tailored." Kate, being experienced, knew exactly what the customer wanted and what size it should be.

Once, when things were urgent and Walter was sick, C.H. wired her in New York: "We are having calls for spring hats. Other stores here are showing them. Think you should try to get some soon as you possibly can and have them forwarded." But other times, C.H., overseeing every transaction as he did, indicated that he was not completely happy with Kate's selections. He sent a wire to Walter, who was in New York, that said, "The first shipment of Kate's dresses came in this morning and eleven of the evening dresses she purchased for $10.50 are not satisfactory…The success of our business depends entirely upon intelligent judgment in selecting our merchandise…It is a difficult business to find the attractive clothes ahead of the competitors." C.H. did not want the ladies' ready-to-wear department to slide backward in sales as it had the previous year. Still, the bottom line was that he did have confidence in her judgment. Kate continued working as a successful buyer until 1943, when she retired.

At Walter's managers' meeting in 1955, just after the buyers had returned from New York, Gertrude McCollam, the longtime and well-respected buyer for women's wear, was quite excited. "We really should have something to tell the customers about this year," she said. "Lilli Ann is going to lead the fashion picture." Mr. Bailey, who worked in men's clothing, had not seen many new fabrics but reported that the big fad in New York was the black-watch plaid. Floyd Alkire in the shoe department had bought more shoes for young girls than older women. But it was Mr. Senter, buyer for the furniture department, who got Walter's attention, as there were lots of new homes going up in Missoula at the time. "Color," Senter reported, "is key. The main trend is towards browns and yellow-greens." The "really high style" was lavender, but he did not buy anything in that color, as he did not think that would suit Missoula.

Judy Baldizar became the buyer for the Bon's ready-to-wear department in 1976 and retired in 1999, right after the store evolved into Bon-Macy's. She worked as a buyer for several of the Allied stores after the

The new bridal department, 1950s. *No. 78-0069, Archives and Special Collections, Mansfield Library, University of Montana.*

consolidation. Among her New York purchases were dresses, evening wear and bridal gowns. The latter was a feature of the Missoula store, as there were no specialty bridal shops in Missoula at the time she was working. The bridal shop was one of the departments added in Walter McLeod's 1950s upgrade of the store. She described buying ten to twenty gowns of every kind for the bridal department. Women came from all over Montana to buy them at the bridal shop. In an interview, she related that the Missoula Mercantile had a furrier, which was also unusual for Missoula.

Consolidation

One of the reasons for the success of the Mercantile was the fact that the Missoula store did do its own buying and knew what its customers wanted. Jim Meyers, the store's general manager after Allied took over in 1959, commented that Allied consolidated its buying in the Seattle store in 1978. The Missoula store became a small fish in a big pond. He explained that the Missoula store always did a great business in coats in the fall, particularly between September 1 and 10, when the store could sell upward of three hundred coats. By September 10, 1978, after the consolidation, it had been sent only ten to twelve coats, and even after urgent phone calls, it only got a few more coats to sell, nothing near what the store had stocked and sold before. Needless to say, it was very understocked and lost money. The bridal department was the exception to the dilemma brought on by consolidation, as the Missoula store benefited from having its employee working as the buyer for all eight of the Allied stores in the region.

However, a far worse thing happened in that consolidation: all the store records of customers were lost, a case history of fifteen thousand accounts. Jim Meyers remembered the chaos that ensued when Allied set up a $100 limit for all customers. "I had people six and seven deep talking to our credit people…and they had been trading here for thirty years…many people came up and cut their cards in two in front of us…It cost us just tons of business."

The Credit Union

The Missoula Mercantile Employees Federal Credit Union was established in August 1937. It was described as providing a means for " promoting thrift among its members and as a source of credit for provident or productive uses." More than one employee got a mortgage for his or her house through the Credit Union. A representative from the Farm Credit Administration came from Washington, D.C., and explained the program to employees who were interested. It was accepted, and the Credit Union still exists today and has 275 members. At one time, Ina Swanson, Gordon's wife, ran it. Today, it is run by Debra Wohl McConaughey, who started at the Mercantile when she was sixteen years old as an elevator operator. She indicated that she had to take a test to get hired. Her father had worked for the Missoula Mercantile Company for forty years, starting in 1944 in the maintenance department.

Trucks and the Mercantile Garage

Joe Menard was head of the Missoula Mercantile's farm implement department in 1901 when he received the first automobile for the company. It was an exciting moment, and although the *Missoulian* did not indicate the make, it anticipated the car would soon be on the street after it was assembled. It was one of the first cars in Missoula, and Joe reportedly said to "set it aside as his personal charge."

Wagons with horses were the first delivery vehicles, but soon, there was a fleet of delivery trucks proudly sporting the Missoula Mercantile's name on the side. Jim Meyers noted there were fifty-eight trucks and a garage with two mechanics (sometimes three) to keep the fleet running. By 1924, the Missoula Mercantile was advertising that it had everything in stock for the auto tourist, from a luggage carrier to a "glare neutralizer." According to Ty Robinson, all of the managers had cars by the end of the 1940s.

Missoula Mercantile delivery truck. *Pictorial Histories Publishing Company.*

The Telephone–Just Call 103

In today's world of cell phones, it is hard to remember when phones were a novelty. A 1913 Mercantile publication advised that there was no need to look up a number: just ask the operator for the Missoula Mercantile exchange. In 1922, the Missoula Mercantile advertised the telephone as a "feature of 'store service,'" to be used when it was inconvenient to visit the store, a feature that "commands every resource of the organization at the end of the wire." The number to dial was 103.

The Missoula Mercantile had a survey done of its facilities sometime before 1934. The result was a list of recommendations for improved telephone service, not only within the store but also with its buildings around town: the warehouses, the cold storage facility, the hay barn, the granary, the salt house and room 406 in the Hammond Building, no doubt Hammond's office.

Playing at the Mercantile: The Reading Room and Sponsored Sports

After the incorporation of the Missoula Mercantile in 1885, a reading room was established for employees in the old Eddy building across the street from the Mercantile. Mrs. Bonner was asked to buy books for this room, and thanks to a newspaper account, we have an idea of the books initially provided. They included both English and French authors but only a couple of Americans: James Fenimore Cooper and Washington Irving, both popular at the time. Although the twelve different sets of books seemed to emphasize the history of France and England, there were twelve volumes of novels by Mary W. Shelley and one volume of Robert Burns's poetry. A ten-volume Chambers's Encyclopedia was also available. Unfortunately, there is no record of how often the reading room was used, and there is no mention of its existence in later years.

Although there is scant information about it, the Missoula Mercantile sponsored teams of various types for its employees. Ray Bailey was a member of a championship indoor baseball team that was sponsored by the Mercantile. A trophy, now at the Historical Museum at Fort Missoula, was presented to the Missoula Mercantile Team, the champions of the Garden City Indoor Baseball League, during the 1911–12 season. Another trophy was sponsored by the Mercantile for the interscholastic track meet, which was won in 1930 by Missoula County High School. In 1922, as evidenced by a letter of thanks to the Mercantile, the company sponsored another community sport, presenting trophies to the Rattlesnake Racket Club, the winners of the Western Montana Tennis Championship Tournament. At several of the early Mercantile company picnics at Riverside Park, a girls' drum and bugle corps is mentioned as participating. A 1929 photo by Missoula photographer R.H. McKay depicts thirty-one men in white shirts and bowties, each bearing a company patch. The photograph is titled the "Missoula Mercantile Bowling Group," but it is not known where the team bowled. Last, and by no means least, the Missoula Mercantile in the 1940s joined with the local Highlander Brewery and sponsored the Highlander baseball team.

Playing at the Mercantile: Picnics and Parties

It was not all work and no play at the Missoula Mercantile. Beginning in the 1920s, there were regular summer picnics for employees. The store closed early for these events. For several years, they were held at Riverside Park, just east of Missoula. Copper baron William Andrews Clark had built this park after he built his hydroelectric dam and the Western Lumber Mill at Riverside (the town would later be renamed Milltown), and it was modeled on his better-known and more extensive park in Butte, Columbia Gardens. Riverside Park was widely used by Missoula citizens and local residents from Riverside and Bonner as the streetcar stopped there on its way to Bonner, but the park faded into oblivion after Clark's death, when the Anaconda Company bought Clark's Western Mill in 1928, only half a mile away from its thriving and larger Bonner Mill.

McLeod employed R.H. McKay to record these events in long panoramic formats. The time needed to take these pictures allowed one small boy to run around to the opposite end, enabling him to appear at both ends of the picture, a copy of which McLeod sent to Hammond (who, thanking McLeod, indicated that it would "find a resting place in [his] office"). The photos show over six hundred people enjoying an afternoon of games and food. Of course, some of them were family members, but the number of actual employees was well over two hundred. Games were organized; baseball, horseshoes and a nail-driving contest for the ladies were popular. C.H. addressed the crowd, ever reminding them of their roles: "The store is not a one-man proposition but the cooperation of the employees, their families and their friends are needed to make the institution great and the people who work for it happy."

In June 1924, employees staged a parade in front of the store on Front Street prior to the picnic, which McKay also photographed. Someone carried a sign saying "Vote for Andy," which has been erroneously interpreted as vote for Hammond. Rather, it appears to refer to the well-known comic strip of the period "The Gumps," as both Andy and his wife, Min, were depicted in the parade.

Over the years, other employee parties would be held annually and often at the Florence, and these events were usually described in the newspapers. One such gathering was held on January 5, 1945, when over five hundred attended as guests of the Missoula Mercantile for a "fine turkey dinner" followed by a vaudeville show. Walter McLeod was the toastmaster and manager of the show. His wife, Olive, who was a trained opera singer, sang as well. It was frequently said that Walter loved to entertain people, so he was in his element at a function like this.

A similar party was given for over seven hundred employees and their families in 1950, when the show revolved around "The Cabaret Tambourine, set some eighteen miles from Algiers," where "Various impersonations of well known Missoula Mercantile personnel were a feature of the dinner hour."

This poem came from an earlier event, probably in the 1920s, but is similar in its frivolity. It is entitled "Herb McCloudsky."

His name is Herb McCloudsky and he runs the M.M. Store
That's where the best of silks are sold. Dat's why they buy some more.
When the ladies want pajumpers and camisoles galore
And shopping bags and stockings they never make him sore.

We've got the nicest ladies and we've got the nicest men
And we got the nicest managers since King Tut-ankh-amen
We've got the best cigar man out where the west begins
His name is Jimmy Busey. He's the El Sidelo king.

There's Walter, He's the manager that travels on the floor
With smiles and nods for everyone that ambles in the door
And Haviland the killer who sends his carpets o're
The state Of Old Montana—he's a salesman to the core.

There's the Barnes and Bailey circus and Lundstrum to be sure
And Eddie Gantt the giant, they're the pirates of the store.
We're just a great big family, two hundred strong or more
And we're boosters for McCloudsky and we're loyal to the core.

Chorus
Oh Missoula Mercantile, Montana's biggest store
Dat's where you buy the goods and then you buy some more—ore
Yes, we ain't got no bananas, but courtesy galore
When you trade with Herb McCloudsky at the great big M.M. store.

These events made working at the Mercantile a fun place to be. That employees liked and respected the two managers was clearly important as well.

Chapter Seven

HELPING THE COMMUNITY HELPS THE STORE

Hammond and the Community

From its earliest times, the Missoula Mercantile was heavily involved in community affairs, primarily those of Missoula. This underlying theme was advocated both by A.B. Hammond and C.H. McLeod, although their motivation often came from different directions. Thus, in 1878, we find Hammond and Richard Eddy among the sponsors of the Third Annual Western Montana Fair as important individuals in the community. By 1928, it is the Missoula Mercantile that is the sponsor, showcasing one-minute washers and a new style of chicken coop at its display booth, as well as an "oil-O-matic" heater in a sample furnace room.

The train that Hammond orchestrated to go to Victor in 1887 carried many dignitaries, who were then wined and dined by Hammond in his effort to win them over to his plans to develop the rich Bitterroot agricultural lands south of Missoula. By May 12, 1910, C.H. McLeod was becoming the voice of the Missoula Mercantile. He rode on William Andrews Clark's new electric streetcar on its inaugural ride through town. The mayor and the editor of the *Missoulian* newspaper were also along for the ride.

Hammond depended on the Missoula Mercantile for his business dealings; money moved in and out of its accounts, but Hammond was not afraid to go all out when he felt that his investments were in danger.

Streetcar in front of the Missoula Mercantile. *Pictorial Histories Publishing Company.*

When banks were failing in 1893, he borrowed $42,000 from the Missoula Mercantile in order to keep the First National Bank from going under. Keeping both the bank and the store afloat was essential in his eyes if the community was to prosper in the long run.

Deciding where the new state capital would be located was perhaps one of the most dramatic attempts to win over the community. It was intertwined with other issues too complicated to delve into here, but to put it simply, copper baron Marcus Daly favored his own town of Anaconda, where he had built his smelter, as the new capital while Hammond backed Helena. Missoula was not in contention; instead of the capital, it wanted to host the state's university, something Hammond wanted as well, but getting Helena was key to this effort. Missoula, however, voted soundly for Anaconda on the first round of votes for the capital, so Hammond dispatched C.H. to the Bitterroot Valley with orders to "manag[e] the distribution of money and liquor for the promise of a vote for Helena." Hammond allocated $7,500 for this effort; Daly spent considerably more, but this time Hammond was successful. Missoula got the university. In another rivalry, Hammond and Higgins each donated twenty acres of their lands south of the river for the building site. The seeds Hammond had sown would grow with the McLeods and the Mercantile, and all three men would be staunch supporters of the university for the rest of their lives. Many times, donation checks would head

Montana State University with Missoula in background. Much of the intervening undeveloped land was owned by Hammond and the Missoula Mercantile. *Photograph A-III_a-034 M, Archives and Special Collections, Mansfield Library, University of Montana.*

to the university to fund this project or that department, and the Missoula Mercantile played a major role in keeping the university alive during World War II. Having the university in town was like having a large town within the borders of the city, and both Hammond and the McLeods knew that.

It is perhaps not surprising that one place where Hammond's name remains intact is the University of Montana, originally named Montana State University. Hammond's daughter Edwina Hammond King, strongly encouraged by Walter McLeod and the then university president Harry K. Newburn, donated money for a chair position in the history department in 1962. As if to complete the circle, her donation came in the form of Missoula Mercantile stock. The Mercantile was once again providing support for the community. The chair was intended for a professor in western history, but initially, it was only sufficient to provide for a summer salary for such a professor in addition to covering some research projects for graduate students. The first chair was K. Ross Toole, followed by H. Duane Hampton, and today, the position is held by Dan Flores.

A Hammond scholarship fund was also established by Mrs. King and provides money to "incoming freshmen in the worthy scholarship program." Her granddaughter, Francis King Field, and her husband, Charles, augmented it through their private foundation in San Francisco, the Field Foundation. It is now, according to the University of Montana Foundation that administers it, "one of UM's largest scholarship funds."

The controversy between Hammond and Daly over the site of the capital had repercussions for the Missoula Mercantile, which lost some of its customers, at least for a while. Daly and Hammond, once both in the Democratic Party, were now on opposite sides after the capital fight, as Hammond had become a Republican. Hammond opted to remain a Republican, which infuriated Daly, who boasted that he would see "the grass grow in the streets of Missoula." Daly even went so far as to withdraw his lucrative contract for mine stulls from Hammond's Bonner Mill and establish his own town of Hamilton in the Bitterroot Valley, complete with its own mill to compete with Hammond's. Daly brought Hennessey's store over from Butte to be a competitor to the Missoula Mercantile, but it was not successful. The Mercantile Company ended up buying out Hennessey's store and its unsold inventory. By 1896, Daly had cut all the wood around his Hamilton Mill, so he attempted to buy Hammond's Bonner Mill. (It was general practice at that time to move out of a mill when the wood nearby was used up.) However, to arrange this deal, Daly preferred to deal directly with Hammond and not C.H. McLeod. To spite him, Hammond raised the price each time Daly complained, and Daly ended up paying almost $1.2 million for the mill, up from the original $750,000 asking price. Daly did, however, also get $500 million worth of board feet of timber in the Blackfoot River drainage in the deal, which was ultimately good for Daly. Although Daly died in 1900, his Anaconda Copper Mining Company (ACM) prospered with the mill, which became the largest sawmill between St. Paul and the West Coast. For unrelated reasons, ACM sold the mill to U.S. Plywood–Champion International in 1972.

In perhaps a surprising turn of events, or maybe it was simply that he was no longer interested in sparring with his old rival now that he had left Missoula, Hammond sold the Bonner Mill to Daly in 1898 and then sold him one-third interest in the Missoula Mercantile. When it came time many years later to liquidate what remained of the Missoula Mercantile, Daly's shares had been passed along many generations.

They had been inherited first by his widow and later his son who, by the time of the liquidation, was also dead, leaving the shares to his fifth wife. Hammond apparently did not mind selling the mill, as it enabled him to concentrate on bigger lumber prospects in Oregon; eventually, California's redwoods would lure him away still farther. He left his home in Missoula in 1894 and only returned for occasional visits thereafter, never to live there or be engaged in Montana's political scene again. He left that to Daly.

The Extended Community

Nevertheless, Hammond's other enterprises within Missoula remained, all of which became the full responsibility of McLeod and the Missoula Mercantile. Hammond had bought up large amounts of land south of the river in Missoula, and as the James Bonner map illustrates, by 1911, there were still many lots marked "Hammond, South Missoula Land Company," or "the Missoula Mercantile Company." They came with restrictions: houses had be built within three years and had to be at least eight hundred square feet in size. McLeod and the Missoula Mercantile were still selling these lots in the late 1940s. Corner lots were $300 and inside lots $200. Indeed, the last four lots would not be disposed of until the 1980s.

Another area in the community that relied on the Missoula Mercantile's support was Fort Missoula, which also developed west of town. The fort was built in 1877, around the same time E.H. & Company started building its store. Since then, an additional fort had been built outside of Helena, not very far away from Missoula. When the political winds moved against Fort Missoula in favor of Fort Harrison, McLeod stepped up to keep the federal contracts and men in Missoula.

Certainly, the Missoula Mercantile Company also played a big role on the Flathead Reservation that was to the north of Missoula. And when, in 1910, the reservation became open for non-Indian settlement (that is, white settlement), the company backed efforts to put sympathetic owners on the land who would in turn become Mercantile customers or even local suppliers if they became involved in agriculture or cattle raising.

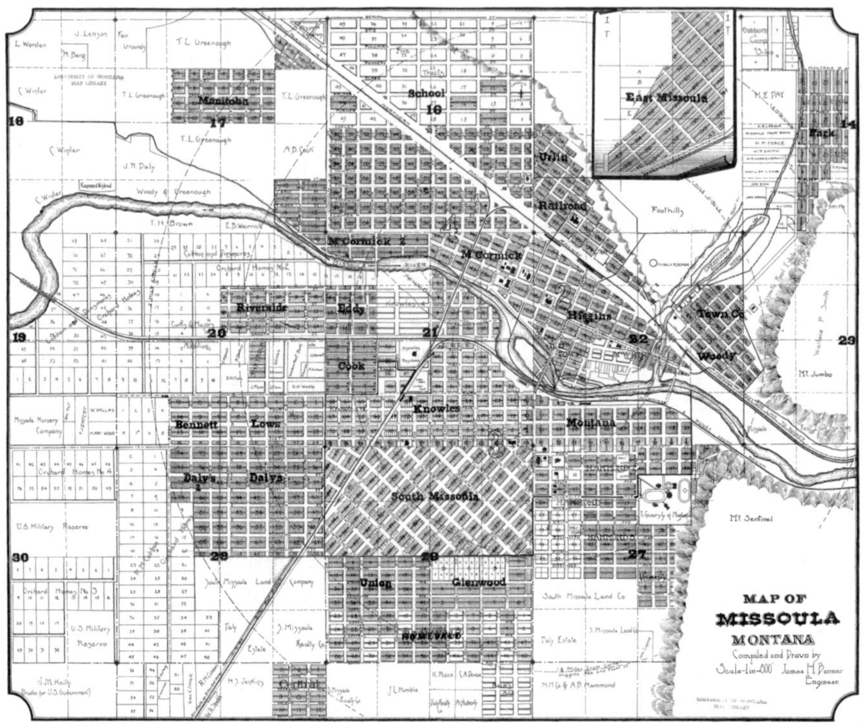

Map of Missoula by James Bonner, 1911. *No. UMT 040004, Archives and Special Collections, Mansfield Library, University of Montana.*

It is then not surprising that a large Flathead Reservation Information Agency was located in Hammond's First National Bank building, as shown in the 1908 postcard on the opposite page. The bank notably opened two years before the reservation.

In a letter written in November 1906 to Hammond's son Richard, C.H. described the business conditions, which are reflective of factors that were affecting the prosperity of western Montana and, thereby, the Mercantile:

> *Our business for the last few months has been better than ever before, and the building of the Milwaukee Road* [RR] *through this country; the double tracking of the Northern Pacific between Garrison and Plains; the opening of the Indian Reservation; the development of mines and the increased timber business will all tend to make this a pretty good country in a business way for a good many years*

Postcard from 1908 showing Higgins Avenue. The Flathead Reservation Information Agency and the First National Bank are on the right, and MMCo is in the next block on the right. *Author's collection.*

> *to come and our business and profits will be much greater in the immediate future than they have been for several years past.*

On the Local Level

On the local level, the presence of the Missoula Mercantile was felt in many, many ways. When C.H. proposed to Hammond that they should donate to the YMCA fund drive in 1910, Hammond concurred that $10,000 "should be our share." St. Patrick's Hospital was another good example. The hospital was opened by the Sisters of Providence in 1873 and was supported for a long time by the Mercantile Company. C.H. had been chairman of the committee when it was building an addition, and although he declined a request to be chair again, he nevertheless pledged Missoula

Mercantile support for "10 percent of an amount that can be raised up to $15,000."

When the Great Forest Fire of 1910 roared through western Montana—burning three million acres in just two days and creating thousands of refugees who managed to get to Missoula only by trains that were racing over burning trestle bridges—C.H. thought nothing of opening the store in the middle of the night when the first load of people arrived at 2:00 a.m. and helped to provide refugees clothing while also sending shovels, pails and axes back on the train to help the firefighting effort. That day, curiously, was the twenty-fifth anniversary of the store known as the Missoula Mercantile.

Both C.H. and Walter were very involved with and supportive of the Boy Scouts. A large ad in the *Missoulian* in 1950 marked the fortieth anniversary of the founding of the national organization. The Mercantile was the local headquarters for scouting, and both equipment and books could be bought there.

C.H. responded to the pleas of duck hunters in Missoula, who were upset that a game preserve that eliminated hunting had been set up by the legislature about 1918 in the Grass Valley area west of Missoula. Landowners had complained that their cattle were being harassed by duck hunters and could not drink water there. Duck hunters who wanted more hunting opportunities sought the power of the Missoula Mercantile (where they got their hunting supplies). In the 1940s, after the Mercantile pressured state legislators, the area was once again opened to hunters. Ironically, too many hunters came, and the ducks left. Today, the hunting rights are leased, and with reduced hunting pressure, the ducks have returned.

The Mercantile Loves a Parade and an Event

Parades were a standard component of life in Missoula and were always well represented by Mercantile floats that oftentimes won prizes for the quality of their decorations and design. In the early days of the twentieth century, floats from different departments competed. In the late 1900s, the cigar and cigarette department's float was, not surprisingly, pulled by a horse, most likely from the company's delivery service. Walter

McLeod was in charge of the historical pageant parade that was held in Missoula on July 5, 1915, to commemorate Missoula's fiftieth birthday. The company float depicted the first mercantile store in Missoula, Worden & Company, instead of its own store, which was, of course, the second.

In 1933, a tractor touting "Farm Power" pulled the Missoula Mercantile entry, a float carrying the familiar wagon and oxen that had been the Eddy and Hammond's logo. Parades, of course, always went by the Missoula Mercantile building on Higgins Avenue, and it was not unusual to see employees watching from the roof. Flags were also often draped across the windows. The Missoula Mercantile building bearing a large white cross, as pictured on page 104, was unusual; however, that parade was related to the six-day joint convention of the Young People's Luther League and the International Youth Foundation, which brought over nine thousand Lutherans from all over the world to Missoula in July 1957.

Several times, the Mercantile closed early to allow customers and employees to attend a community event such as the high school track meet in 1930. Missoula County School won the event. The store was always closed for Decoration Day (now called Memorial Day), as well as the Fourth of July. The only exception was in 1933, when July Fourth fell on a Tuesday, and the governor belatedly had declared Monday a holiday as well. The Mercantile explained in an ad why it was staying open on the Monday: "Our employees generally are in hearty accord with this arrangement in view of the fact that all are to have at least a three-day vacation with full pay this season."

The Missoula Mercantile worked hand in hand with its subsidiary, the Florence Hotel. All its major events were held in its banquet rooms, and important visitors to town like Theodore Roosevelt, John Wayne and Gary Cooper always stayed there. Employees often had lunch in the Florence coffee shop, which was added when the hotel was rebuilt a second time. An anticipated event for the ladies in the 1950s was the style show luncheon series, a four- to five-fashion show event and lunch (all for $1.35 each) that showed off the latest in women's and children's fashions. Miss Ray, one of the Mercantile's head secretaries in the 1950s, wrote to Walter McLeod, "As usual I went to the hotel during my lunch hour and the third Missoula Mercantile Company Style Show was taking place. Two hundred and seventy people were present and there were fourteen tables in the lobby." She noted that one well-dressed lady had commented, "These style shows have certainly made me clothes conscious."

Missoula Mercantile float in 1933 parade. *No. 001-VIII_78-07_051, Archives and Special Collections, Mansfield Library, University of Montana.*

Parade for Young People's Luther League, 1957. *No. 90-2182, Archives and Special Collections, Mansfield Library, University of Montana.*

Photograph of Walter McLeod and Gary Cooper discussing fishing equipment. *No. 002-XXVI_008_WMcLeod_G. Cooper, Archives and Special Collections, Mansfield Library, University of Montana.*

The Store in the Community: The MISCO Grain Department

The Missoula Feed and Grain Company (MISCO) was set up as a separate department of the Missoula Mercantile Company in 1921 to serve a growing need for the distribution of grain in western Montana. It brought farmers and ranchers all over the western part of the state into the company's domain, creating a huge agricultural market.

Initially it had four employees, but by 1939, there were fifty, with five branches in western Montana: Deer Lodge, Bozeman, Kalispell, Ronan and Hamilton. Charles Quinn worked for this department from 1921 to 1952, many of those years as manager. Mercantile's advertising claimed that the dramatic increase in Montana poultry raising was entirely due to MISCO's efforts. Feed, advice and information were available to farmers and ranchers for every type of livestock. The department, in 1939, purchased fifty to sixty thousand bushels of wheat and several million pounds of oats, "contributing much to the wealth, progress and prosperity of agriculture in the territory." The company had grain elevators at Clyde Park (near Livingston), Ronan, Charlo and Pablo. In 1935, the Mercantile bought two elevators and a feed mill in Bozeman, and in 1939, C.H. wrote one of the branch managers that the company had just bought three elevators on the Flathead Reservation for $6,000 each, which, he added, "was just 20 percent of their original cost." MISCO also bought and cleaned local seeds and distributed them to the East. Not knowing the deadly effects at the time, a MISCO flier offered Aerosol DDT bombs in 1947, surplus from the U.S. Government, for $37.50 a dozen.

The Mercantile as the Community Bank

On another level, the Mercantile benefited the community by often serving as its unofficial bank. Both McLeods (but particularly C.H.) made a habit of keeping considerable cash in the twelve-foot vault on the second floor. A special compartment that contained an amount close to $30,000 was always available for "donations" (particularly political) or just helping someone out. Also, managers would get an extra $20,000 to $30,000 on Fridays to "carry people over," by cashing their personal checks. According to Ty Robinson, when he came in 1948, there were "millions in the vault." Needless to say, he was astonished.

Jim Meyers noted in his oral history that they got very few bad checks. In one instance, C.H. wrote to a former employee, Mrs. B. who had lost property in the 1906 San Francisco earthquake, that he would give her a note for $100 to help her out but that "as soon as possible she should start sending in $10.00 to go against it." McLeod was a good judge of character, and most of the time these loans were paid back.

Meyers added that the management was generally quiet about its political donations; they didn't want it known who they were supporting. "You know it wasn't just a couple of hundred dollars, it was tens and fifteen thousands of dollars," Meyers said. In a talk he gave on Missoula history in 2010, Ty Robinson said that when he came to work as an attorney for the Mercantile, he was given an office next to Walter McLeod, and early on, he noticed a trail of prominent visitors each week: the chairman of the Republican Party, the chair of the Democratic Party, the chief of police and the fire department chief, followed by all three members of city council. Apparently, they all came to get their marching orders or at least be kept in the loop. One day, Robinson was asked to deliver a check to Missoula's chamber of commerce, whose annual budget was around $32,000 at that time. The check was for $20,000!

Mercantile Employees Help the Community

The Missoula Mercantile had a good workforce and, from time to time, wanted to remind the community of this fact. An ad in 1937 did just that as it proclaimed that after seventy-two years, the store had 275 regular employees who, with their families and dependents, aggregated "644 persons who draw their support from this store." The statistics that followed informed the public of the contribution to the community these folks made: 35 percent owned their own homes, 60 percent owned automobiles, 80 percent contributed to churches, 48 percent belonged to lodges and clubs and 92 percent contributed to welfare organizations. And for their ultimate contribution, all of these persons paid $16,762.41 in taxes. Not only was the Missoula Mercantile a stable institution, but its employees were also part of what made Missoula a strong community.

Christmas at the Missoula Mercantile

For many in Missoula, Christmas at the Missoula Mercantile was a very special time, as the reader can judge from a few random memories. The store was decorated, inside and out. Santa Claus was annually stationed in the shoe department, and Toy Lane went from the hardware department to shoes through the glassware department (much to the objections of the glassware personnel!). The toy department temporarily reappeared annually, except for the year of 1930. It may come as a surprise that toys were not a regular department in the store until the 1950s reorganization, when the "Toy Deck" was established in a mezzanine between the first and second floors. Walter saw the 1930 lapse as a mistake and asked his sister Helen in Chicago if she could not find at least some dolls and send them to the store. They needed to be competitive with the "Madam Hendron dolls" that were available at another department store in town. He perhaps had a personal motive, as his daughter, Clara Marsh, particularly wanted a "Patsy Ann doll dressed in green organdie."

Dennis Sain remembered that KB dolls were the hot item during Christmas in 1958. They were stored in the basement in a space that was actually under the Front Street sidewalk, and he had to continually go up and down the stairs to resupply the Toy Deck with this item. A Santa Claus mask sold at the Toy Deck and stamped with the company name is now at the Historical Museum at Fort Missoula.

In 1908, the *Missoulian* reported that most of the stores stayed open until midnight on Christmas Eve. Chauncey Woodworth, who would grow up to be a Missoula photographer and surveyor for the Northern Pacific, was just a little boy at the time, and the *Missoulian* reported that he was interested in the Shetland pony that the Missoula Mercantile was displaying. It was not clear whether the animal was real or a toy.

In the late 1940s, a watchful photographer caught a woman shoplifting before Christmas, which made a stir in the local newspaper. The photo showed that the store was packed.

Walter, writing to his sister Helen on December 1, 1928, described the early days of the "Christmas rush." Toyland had opened "with all its difficulties." Although he does not describe this, no doubt it had to do with the Lionel electric train that everyone had been looking forward to.

> *We have a wonderful window piece, called "The Mill in the Lonely Dell," which is a little village scene filled with dolls. The felt kind and they are flaying grain, shoeing horses, washing, cutting wood, etc... We have found that the grownups love it more than the children, and we feel it is a real attraction and "big city" stuff.*

The comparison to big cities had been part of the unspoken goals of the Missoula Mercantile from its beginnings as E.H. & Company; somehow, being more like eastern stores or carrying goods available in the East was felt to give the store more credibility. Hence, they were especially pleased when the Missoula Mercantile earned a national award in 1943 for its Christmas window, designed by store display manager Raymond Reed and cited for its use of illumination. The award came from the International Association of Displaymen, and there were several thousand entries.

On a final Christmas note, customers came from all over to shop at the Mercantile for Christmas. A grand piano was brought in, and it was a fun and festive experience, as expressed by Mrs. Davis, who wrote from Polson after her Christmas shopping visit, "I want to tell you how very much I enjoyed the singing of Christmas carols. It was so warm and neighborly, so friendly."

Community Thoughts About the Mercantile

Perhaps the important question that should be asked at this point is what did the community think of the Missoula Mercantile? Certainly during Hammond's last days in the town, many were raising questions about the octopus that seemed to have grown in their midst. By contrast, there was the dinner given for C.H. McLeod in 1933 on the fiftieth anniversary of his arrival in Missoula. Over five hundred people attended to honor him, as the toastmaster said, "Because we like you Herb McLeod." The speakers included Governor Erickson, the chancellor of the university, as well as dignitaries from across Montana. It was hosted by the chamber of commerce and three service clubs—the Kiwanis Club, the Rotary Club and the Lions—and was held in the gym of Loyola School. The paper gave special mention of the speech of Boy Scout Robert Grantier, who said that without McLeod's help, the Boy Scout movement would have failed many times in western Montana. The entire guest list was included in the paper, as were many of the hundreds of telegrams received. A.B. Hammond's telegram, almost predictably, stated he had other "urgent business engagements," but in the letter, he did commemorate McLeod's "loyal friendship and invaluable assistance." What seemed most fitting was that this tribute to C.H. came during his lifetime and not after his death.

C.H. was awarded two honorary degrees by the university, both of which he declined as he did not think himself worthy of them. In addition to the plaque in the Florence building honoring C.H., there is a McLeod Street in the university district of Missoula that is named for him. In 1921, the U.S. Board of Geographical Names named a mountain summit in the Rattlesnake Wilderness north of Missoula for the man who managed the Missoula Mercantile. McLeod Peak, at 8,620 feet, is the highest peak in the wilderness.

Some Last Words from the Community

The community observed the passing of each of the three men who had contributed greatly to the Missoula Mercantile in slightly differently ways. Editorials accompanied obituaries about each.

Andrew Hammond, who died on January 15, 1934, was described in an editorial as the "last of the industrial giants of the west." He was eighty-six years old. Most of the editorial highlights his lumber empire in California, but it does say, "The effects of his organizational genius are still plain in Missoula," concluding, "He was a man who asked no odds of anyone, who determined his objective and pressed toward it with single purpose."

Charles Herbert McLeod died September 5, 1946, at the age of eighty-seven and was hailed for what he did for Missoula and western Montana. "All he did for the community and region will never be known, but it was a great deal. Sense of civic duty was deep within him, and he never shirked what he considered proper responsibility," wrote the editor of the *Missoulian*.

Finally, Walter Herbert McLeod came to his end on September 13, 1963, at the age of seventy-five. The editorial accompanying his obituary described him as "untiringly interested in the progressive development of Montana and for many years was in the forefront of every movement which he considered in that direction." Known as "Mr. Missoula," Walter was sent off by an overflowing church.

All of these men had been members of Missoula's Holy Spirit Episcopal Church, a church whose membership included the Hammonds and the McLeods, as well as the Keith and Beckwith families, all New Brunswick Protestants. Andrew and Florence Hammond were founding members, and Andrew was on the Mission Committee in 1877 when it was first established. Several of the McLeods and Keiths served on the vestry. The Hammonds remained active supporters of the church, and all of their six children were baptized there. In 1956, when the church was adding a parish house, the Church Guild Room was established as a memorial to both Mr. and Mrs. Hammond. The plaque reads, "In memory of A.B. Hammond, Florence Hammond, Jean Keith McLeod, and Annie B. Briggs by Florence Whiteside and George B. McLeod." (Jean was C.H.'s granddaughter, and Annie was A.B.'s niece, the daughter of his sister Sarah. Florence Whiteside was the Hammonds' daughter, and George was C.H.'s cousin who ran the Hammond Lumber Company for many years after Hammond's son Leonard had died.) They were all family, and many are buried in the Missoula Cemetery, which was at one time controlled by A.B. Hammond. Hammond himself is buried in San Francisco.

Chapter Eight

GETTING THE MESSAGE OUT

Early Media Coverage

Since the earliest days of E.H. & Company, advertising played an important part in the company's marketing strategy, if we can apply modern jargon to the prominent ads that appeared in the *Missoulian* as early as January 1877. These ads had no illustrations, and little information was provided, just that the store carried "Boots & Shoes, Hats & Caps, Groceries, Liquors," as well as "long and short legged rubber boots etc." Much was left to the imagination.

By August 1878, E.H. & Company ads were much more detailed, and the company's range of goods had expanded broadly. For example, as part of a long list, it offered items including three hundred sacks of sugar, twenty boxes of sweet crackers, twenty-five kits of mackerel and one hundred kits of codfish. Ladies could find boots and an extensive array of fabric from denim to cashmere, as well as ribbons and dress goods. There was also a full and complete stock of stationery, saddlery, patent medicines and sporting goods, to say nothing of local wheat, flour, hams and cheese. To bolster the ad, a small notice in the "Local Mention" column informed readers: "An ox train of ten wagons with goods for J.P. Reinhard and Eddy Hammond & Company, got in last Saturday."

With the store expanding, E.H. & Company offered a "Grand Display!" in early 1880 and focused on goods that would have more appeal to the woman of the family. "Alpacas, Mohairs, Cashmeres, followed by Plain and fancy colored water proofs, and Lace curtains," proclaimed an ad. That the company sold Main and Winchester saddles and was the agent for "the celebrated Mitchell Wagons" was mentioned at the bottom. Under Stevensville news, a special article stated that Eddy Hammond & Company teams would arrive from the Terminus in Corinne, Utah, in thirteen days with "tons of goods to be sprinkled liberally among their houses in this country." This was a quick time for goods to be delivered from where the Union Pacific Railroad brought them from the East Coast to Montana.

In May 1882, there was an ad that indicated E.H. & Company had gotten into the land business. Ranches were advertised after men's clothing. A Woodman ranch of 480 acres was described, just four miles from Fort Missoula. A second one was in Stevensville. But it was in June that E.H. & Company announced the really big news that would set it apart from the merchandising competition: "$100,000 worth of goods just received in the Missoula Store." The ad, published on June 30, explained:

> *We are now receiving weekly shipments of staple goods direct from Eastern manufacturers in straight carload lots and can supply the wholesale and retail trade in quantities to suit. Having a resident buyer in New York we are in a position to take advantage of any declines in the market and can offer our customers and the public superior inducements in the way of goods at low prices and strictly one price. We have branches at Weeksville, Stevensville, Corvallis and the Flathead Agency. We are agents for the Bain Wagons, the Mitchell wagons, the Champion Reapers and Mowers, the Tiger Sulky Horse Rake and the Oliver Chilled Plow. We pay cash for Hides, Furs and all kinds of country produce.*

In July, the *Missoulian* noted that the Weeksville store needed two clerks to manage its increasing trade, largely from the men constructing the railroad. Bringing the East to the West seems to have been the goal of this growing mercantile enterprise. By 1883, E.H. & Company was advertising itself as a "Bazar [*sic*] of Fashion," offering elegant silverware, beautiful toilet sets, sealskin caps, handsome fur sets and not a few but a "splendid line of ladies French kid shoes." Shortly after the Northern Pacific reached Missoula in September 1883, E.H. & Company received its first freight

Reoccurring etching of Missoula Mercantile showing the earliest store on the present site, the farm implement store in the Elks Temple and the annex across the street that housed the furniture and carpet departments. Earlier versions of this etching feature horse and buggies instead of automobiles and the streetcar. *The Macy's Collection, 2010.003.098. Used by Permission. All Rights Reserved.*

car worth of goods from the East. This was unusual, as most mercantile businesses did not buy by the rail car. By November that year, E.H. & Company was building a brick warehouse that was thirty by one hundred feet and had a platform around the building used as a storehouse and wholesale department. The article described this building as a place where "unbroken packages will be kept, ready for shipment at a moments notice either up or down the road."

In 1885, the Missoula Mercantile ran the following ad: "We are determined to undersell for the same quality of goods any House in the territory and we are in a position to do it." This was the strategy of Andrew Hammond, ably assisted by C.H. McLeod and a growing cadre of loyal employees at the Missoula store and its several branches.

The Commercial Leviathan

Although advertising made it appear that business was booming, there was a cloud lurking in the offing, as government officials were growing more concerned that E.H. & Company, with its lucrative cutting contract with the Northern Pacific, was in fact cutting trees illegally on public domain. Hammond, always professing innocence in this regard, nevertheless sought to protect the huge mercantile interests by reorganizing the entities that held his assets. As noted, it was then that the corporation reorganized, splitting off the lumber business from the merchandising by creating the Missoula Mercantile Company.

The day before the store changed its name, it ran an ad in the *Missoulian* that was blank except for the words "The Missoula Mercantile Company." The ad remained the same size. The next day, the ad announced, "Grand Fall Opening! Missoula Mercantile Company—Successors to Eddy Hammond & Company. We have just opened a magnificent variety of Fall and Winter Dress Goods at Bottom Prices—Silks and Satins and Velveteens!"

Ads now frequently mentioned that the store had its own buyer, which was an unusual feature of a western store. Undoubtedly, Bonner's early experience with Lord and Taylor in New York was useful in pushing E.H. & Company in that direction, and the buyers for the Mercantile were a long-standing feature of the store.

By 1890, Hammond had established the *Missoula Gazette*, a newspaper to rival the *Missoulian*. Having his own paper provided Hammond with an easy opportunity to discuss and advertise the Missoula Mercantile. Personal columns discussed the comings and goings of employees: "Herb Harrison, acting treasurer of the Missoula Mercantile returned yesterday from a 2-week vacation in the Flathead Country and is again at his post of duty." Often these columns shamelessly advertised the activities of the Mercantile in glowing terms:

> *The Missoula Mercantile Company is gladdening the hearts of the farmers and producers of the Bitterroot and Flathead valleys by purchasing their crops of hay, wheat, oats, barley and potatoes and it is estimated that this company will expend this fall fully $100,000 in these purchases.*

Front-page stories carried etchings of the Mercantile in its various stages, recapped its history and provided readers with biographies of the

Postcard of the store issued by the Missoula Mercantile in 1919. *Pictorial Histories Publishing Company.*

major owners and department heads. In December 1890, the twenty-fifth anniversary of the beginning of the business was observed. By that time, capital stock had grown to $600,000, and the company employed 125 people and had a monthly payroll of $30,000. The *Gazette* in both its Missoula and Coeur d'Alene, Idaho editions called the Missoula Mercantile Company "the Commercial Leviathan of the Great Northwest, [a] Business Corporation whose transactions exceed $3,000,000 per year," the main store having $2 million in transactions and the branch stores $1 million. At that time, there were branch houses at Corvallis, Stevensville, Victor and Demersville.

The Missoula store now had eight departments, each with its own head: C.A. Barnes, clothing; C.A. Jones, boot and shoe; T.B. Thompson, grocery; T.J. Jenkins, furniture; Joe Menard, agricultural implement; W.S. Settle, dry goods; Fred Sterling, hardware; and W.S. Mentrum, liquor, which was located across the street from the Mercantile in the first floor of the First National Bank. In addition to C.H. McLeod and Hammond, most of the above came from Canada; only Menard hailed from Quebec, while the rest came from New Brunswick. Jones came from England, while three called the states of Vermont, Virginia and Kentucky home. McLeod, Sterling and Thompson had been working for the Mercantile the longest at that time.

By this time, the Missoula Mercantile also had a growing number of warehouses around town and a three-story annex in the Elks Lodge, across Pattee Street in Missoula, where the agricultural implement department had plenty of space to house large equipment. The Missoula Mercantile had bought the lodge building from T.C. Powers of Helena, and the Elks maintained meeting rooms in the building.

Two years later, the *Missoula Gazette* gave another glowing report on the growing company. The paper attributed the success of the company to its ability "to take advantage of existing favorable conditions, making the best of them, creating and assisting in building up enterprises that give promise of extending the field of trade and enlarging the scope of business operations." The *Gazette* article noted that all of the managers were young men. "Even President Hammond is just beyond 40," it said. Good training and expertise were essential.

The *Gazette* didn't suggest that no other company could do it, but in 1892, it did suggest that inputs of capital into businesses are just as important for the development of the West as, say, the railroads. "This is the age of progress, and new modes of thought and action and new modes of business are required," one article proclaimed. Strategies such as dealing directly with the manufacturer, making yearly contracts and buying by the trainload allowed the Mercantile to effectively compete with eastern markets and brought prestige to Missoula as a wholesale town. The amount of capital allowed it to give credit to struggling farmers or small merchants. "The books of this company show great indulgence to creditors," said the *Gazette*. "Many thousands of dollars are carried year after year and every possible opportunity was given to those involved, whether by their own wild ventures or by circumstances beyond their control, to extricate themselves."

An Advertising Manager

By 1906, the store had an advertising manager. The job fell to Edward Boos, who held it until he died suddenly thirty-one years later. He had been a photographer for the *Daily Missoulian*, and for one assignment in 1897, he followed the U.S. Army Twenty-fifth Infantry on its infamous bicycle tour from Fort Missoula to St. Louis, bringing back photos that confirmed how ill suited bicycles were for army transportation. In the seemingly Hammond tradition, he married Annie Hammond, another of A.B.'s cousins. (She was the daughter of Sophie Coombes, Andrew's aunt, and Brad Hammond, a cousin.)

One of Boos's first assignments at the Missoula Mercantile was for the *Commercial Bulletin and Northwest Trade Journal*, for which he penned an article called "An Interesting Montana Establishment." He incorporated photographs of various departments, such as rug and carpets, which, in 1906, was its own department. The total number of departments by that year had reached twelve and included millinery and cloaks, crockery, tinware, carpets and vehicles. The size of the retail stores was now measured in acres, 3.5 for the three retail stores (Missoula, Kalispell and Victor) and 4 acres for fifteen warehouses. There was only one grain elevator at that time. Two hundred employees were on the payroll, which was then $150,000 per year.

Boos explained that buying in large quantities required selling in large quantities. "Being recognized as jobbers in the trade and by shipping goods in car lots as much as possible instead of locally we are able to compete successfully in our territory with the largest houses in the country," he wrote.

In the jobbing business, they used a combination of traveling salesmen and a catalog. This loose-leaf catalog started out with twelve pages and quickly grew to over eight hundred and was a well-known sales piece across western Montana. Prices included both wholesale and retail. Using a program of rotation, the client was visited once every two weeks.

The New Wall of Windows

To encourage retail sales, the Missoula Mercantile relied primarily on newspaper advertising, window displays and mailed circulars. The company held sales on a regular basis. Window displays were key. Indeed, in 1905, the Missoula Mercantile turned the brick wall on Higgins Avenue into a row of windows that measured one hundred feet long, unusual for any store, particularly in the West. A few years later, Luxfer prisms were placed above

Nighttime photo of the Missoula Mercantile at Christmastime, circa 1946. *No. 70-119, Archives and Special Collections, Mansfield Library, University of Montana.*

them, which transferred the light into the interior of the store and thereby reduced the need for electric lights. A whole new venue was opening up. The new window also signified the changing street use pattern from Front Street to the now more popular Higgins Avenue as the main route through town. The window was opened on October 26, 1905, with a grand announcement and a display of hidden electric lights that gave "light and brightness where before stood a dull and unattractive wall…[It's] a show piece of which Missoula might well be proud."

Shortly before the opening of the new window, a brief note in the *Missoulian* advises that L.N. Simons, another merchant on Higgins, was also having a "handsome" new front installed to "be in line with a number of other merchants along Higgins," so clearly the Mercantile was keeping up with or surpassing its neighbors. Still, this major change to the store is interesting in light of the correspondence between Hammond and McLeod earlier in that year, when Hammond complained about McLeod having spent almost $10,000 on window trimming and advertising. Although the ever-canny Hammond said, "I do not want you to think that I wish to find fault or interfere with the manner in which you conduct your business," he

Window display, fall 1900. *No. 83-0093, Archives and Special Collections, Mansfield Library, University of Montana.*

concluded with, "It will probably do not harm to look them [the figures] over and see if some retrenchment can be made."

McLeod, in a calm manner, carefully explained the expenses: "Window trimming is an important part of the mercantile business today," noting that some similar businesses employed two men to take care of their windows, each at the salary of the Mercantile's one man. McLeod also commented on the amount of advertising in the *Missoulian* and how important it was to support the paper so that a good paper would continue to exist. His reasoning extended to the fact that the Flathead Reservation was due to be opened up to white homesteading, which would bring a lot of new people to the area. The implication was that because of the Missoula Mercantile's interest in Missoula and on the reservation, it behooved the Mercantile to keep a high profile.

Special Coverage

In addition to regular daily advertising, anniversaries of the Missoula Mercantile were always recognized in newspaper ads, although they sometimes went back to the start of the first business of Bonner & Welch on Front Street in 1866, sometimes to the building on its present location (1877) and sometimes to the incorporation of the Missoula Mercantile in 1885. The latter was the case in August 1910, when an ad marked the twenty-fifth anniversary of the store.

A souvenir edition of the *Daily Missoulian* provided another opportunity. On July 20, 1922, the paper welcomed the National Editorial Association to Missoula. The two-page ad touts the reasons of the company's commercial success: "Integrity, Fairness, Progressiveness, Foresightedness and Liberality." Integrity was incorporated into the logo for a number of years following this. In July 1942, the Missoula Mercantile reminded readers that through war and peace and uncertain times, the Mercantile had been there to supply their needs. The ad was more somber and urged people to buy war bonds. (Curiously, this ad dates the company's beginnings back to 1867, not 1866.) This ad prompted an editorial by *Missoula County Times* editor C.J. Doherty, who reflected back on the seventy-five years of the store's existence and its efforts to aid the development of western Montana. "Every city on this section [area], every irrigation project, every form of improvement has been aided by the institution known as the Missoula Mercantile Company."

Doherty noted the thousands of dollars given to charity, religious and educational institutions and thousands more advanced to help individuals in trouble. These were areas he thought that the Mercantile would be unlikely to mention itself, although as seen when Hammond owned the *Missoula Gazette*, he was not reticent about tooting his own horn. Doherty attributed much of the success of the Missoula Mercantile to C.H. McLeod, whose door was always open to those who wanted to talk with him or get help from him.

An article in the *Missoulian* in 1935 recounted that the Missoula Mercantile had been a consistent advertiser for sixty years—the whole of the paper's existence. That was not an accident on the part of the company and, no doubt, contributed to its success and longevity. As two small examples, an ad in 1944 told readers that the Missoula Mercantile now had an office in New York City. "Up-to-the-minute fashions are in our store as quickly as they are in the great shops of Fifth Avenue," it read. It was a not-so-subtle reminder that the Missoula Mercantile was not just an ordinary western department store. Still, in 1942, an ad in the *Missoulian* claimed, "The Mercantile is prepared to supply the stockman with everything but the horse!" The small print reminded the reader that the Mercantile had been serving the stockman's needs for more than seventy-five years. It was happy to remind customers of it western roots.

Community Advertising

The Missoula Mercantile also took advantage of the radio media. In 1939, a regular KGVO radio program called *Builders of Business* featured the store chain's grain department. The grain department had been established in 1921 and had been a consistent advertiser ever since, airing the MISCO Market Report every day at 12:50 p.m.

One area of advertising that seemed to work well for the Mercantile was its regular ads in the university newspaper (*Kaimen*) and the high school papers, as well as the school yearbooks. Through these ads, the company broadened its community outreach and, at the same time, brought younger clientele into the store for shopping. An ad in the September 14, 1914 edition of the *Kaimen* appealed to students directly by describing what students would find interesting about the store. Other ads highlighted the fashion of the day for both young men and women, such as the one in the 1920s that was published in the University of Montana's literary magazine, *The Frontier*. The ad was directed at the "sweet girl graduate" and showed "graduation frocks" that were described as "airy bits of loveliness," dresses that were sure to please.

On the one hand, it was good for business, but on the other, it represented the strong community support that C.H. had brought to the Mercantile. The difference between A.B. Hammond and C.H. McLeod is clear. A.B. tended to look at community investments by bottom line only, while C.H., who *was* the store at the community level, also looked at how the community viewed the store and reached out to be part of the community that had been the cornerstone of his sixty-plus years at the Mercantile. One has only to glance down the list of Missoula Mercantile advertising expenses in the

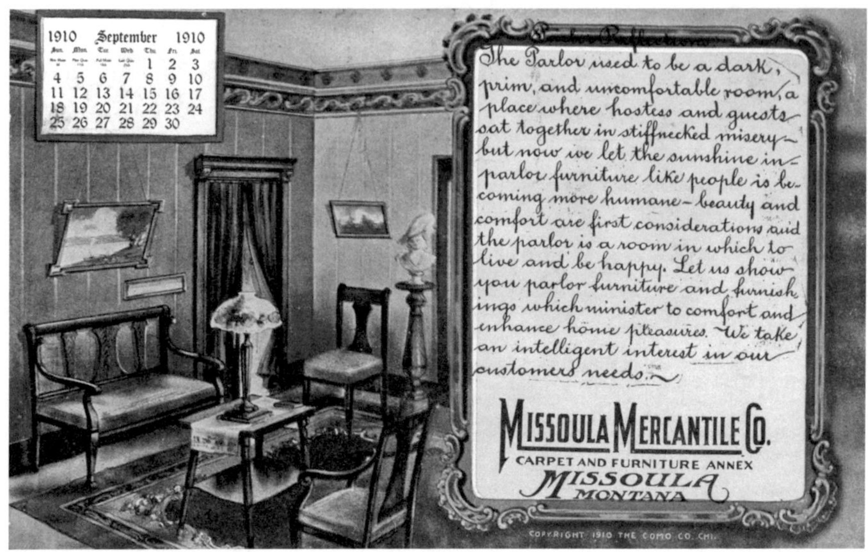

Missoula postcard advertisement featuring a September 1910 calendar. *Pictorial Histories Publishing Company.*

C.H. McLeod had photographer R.H. McKay take many pictures of the Missoula Mercantile. Shown here is the store in 1927 when it was painted white. *Pictorial Histories Publishing Company.*

1920s to see the range of advertising and observe how McLeod's philosophy was implemented. The Mercantile Company had a presence on the national level, being featured in the *Christian Science Monitor* and the *Railway Yardmasters of America*, as well as on the local level: on the local baseball park fence, in local programs such as Swedish concerts and the Missoula Lutheran Church and even in the *InterMountain Educator* and the *Boy Scout Camp Book*. The list was extensive. The various county fairs in Missoula, Sanders and Ravalli, where there were stores, were prime opportunities for displays and mentions in the programs.

Walter McLeod, who took over the store in 1941 when his father retired, made home movies of several of the fairs in the 1930s, which showed the fine displays of McCormick-Deering tractors that the Mercantile sold in its farm implement department. The displays were always crowded.

In addition to the regular publications, the Mercantile ads appeared on the Montana State University blotters; small leather-bound diaries and notebooks were handed out to good customers in the hardware department; and of course, ads appeared on the menus in the Florence Hotel coffee shop.

The Historical Museum at Fort Missoula holds many actual items that the Mercantile sold, embossed with the corporate name. A folding buttonhook for ladies' shoes was given away as "compliments of the Missoula Mercantile Company." Similarly, a tape measure and a needle threader were also given away. When a man received a Stetson hat as a gift from the Mercantile, he was given a miniature Stetson hat in a box. He could bring it to the store and then be measured for his actual hat. Both the hat and the box were marked with the Missoula Mercantile Company logo. Theodore Haviland china from Limoges, France, was a popular item offered under the Missoula Mercantile name, as were Jantzen swimming suits and, in the early days, Neverslip horseshoes and warranted pure-silk fishing line. There were many more such items. It was good advertising.

Chapter Nine

WALTER'S STORE

The Early Years

Walter Herbert McLeod was, from his birth, the heir apparent to the Missoula Mercantile, yet aside from the fact that he grew up in the store, he had received little formal training as to how to actually run a department store or the many businesses he found himself involved in after his father retired.

His counterpart on the Hammond side was Andrew's only living son, Leonard, who took over from his father as head of the vast Hammond Lumber Company in 1934 after Hammond died. Several years before Walter's father, C.H., retired, Leonard wrote to Walter (who was vice-president by then), urging him to get himself appointed as president so that he could have the advantage of his father's wisdom while he was still alive. This was not to be, however. C.H. did not relinquish the reins easily, and it was only after he became ill in June 1941 that he considered retirement, which did not actually happen until December of that year.

Walter, the oldest child of C.H. and Clara McLeod, had a sister named Helen and a younger brother who died at birth. He was not always well growing up and was even sent to a sanitarium in California for several months. He married Olive Wheeler from California on April 5, 1915, and it would be Olive who would suffer nervous breakdowns in later years and

Photograph of the Mercantile, circa 1940s, when Walter McLeod took over management. *No. 70-0120, Archives and Special Collections, Mansfield Library, University of Montana.*

spend months at a time away from home recovering. Nevertheless, they had three healthy children: Olive Brewster, Walter H. Jr. (known as Bud) and Clara Marsh. Twelve grandchildren eventually followed, including Clara Marsh's seven sons. Although Bud worked at the Kalispell store for a time, none of the others had any kind of "official" role in the store, aside from holding shares in the company, thus effectively ending the McLeod "dynasty" at the Missoula Mercantile.

Growing up, Walter and Helen spent time at their father's property, which was called the Hoblitt Ranch, in Victor, Montana. C.H. wrote to a friend in 1910, saying, "Mrs. McLeod and the children are up the Bitterroot at the present. I am interested in quite a large ranch in that section, and they enjoy very much going to the country." The ranch, of course, was part of Hammond's scheme to encourage development in the Bitterroot. C.H. made sure that the family connection there continued as Walter and Helen would, in time, be tied legally not only to the ranch as stockholders but to the Victor Land and Livestock Company, Hammond's development company in the Bitterroot.

Although the family maintained the ranch property for some years after World War II, Walter and Helen also built cabins far away from the Bitterroot on the west side of Seeley Lake on land leased from the Forest Service. They were one of the first of many Missoula families to do so. It was there that the extended family gathered for a great many years. The women and the children would stay for months in the summer while their husbands came up from Missoula with fresh supplies on the weekends. As Jo Rainbolt's *Missoula Valley History* describes, C.H. and Walter delivered the Saturday night edition of the *Missoulian* to any Mercantile customers along the route to Seeley Lake, tooting their automobile horn to tell the ranchers their paper had arrived.

Having a close getaway must have eased family tensions: Walter had sometimes found it difficult to get a few days' vacation from his workaholic father and the store. C.H. also found the Seeley Lake cabins a rest, although he sometimes brought work with him in the form of prominent guests. Perhaps the most famous was Charles Lindbergh, who was on a national tour in 1927, just two months after his record-breaking flight across the Atlantic. McLeod provided what was described as a "sumptuous" lunch at Seeley Lake before the party rode on to the summer cabin of John Ryan, president of the Anaconda Copper Mining Company, on Elbow Lake. That lake was later renamed Lindbergh Lake by the Anaconda Company.

First Jobs at the Store

In high school, Walter often worked weekends and vacations at the store. He started college at Montana State University in Missoula but left in 1911 to become a full-time clerk at the Missoula Mercantile, so he never graduated. Nevertheless, throughout his career, he promoted the university, maintaining a close relationship with its various presidents. He would be awarded the Montana State University's Distinguished Service Alumni Award in 1962, but that was many years away.

In 1915, Walter was promoted to floorwalker, watching over the various departments and directing customers. Five years later, he became vice-president but did not have many responsibilities. His correspondence addressed store inquiries and employment requests but nothing major.

In 1928, C.H. wrote to Walter, already age forty-one, as if he was advising a much younger man. Walter was in New York on some unexplained mission for the store. C.H. wrote:

> *We received your letter yesterday and are glad to know you have met so many prominent people since you have been in New York...You perhaps will realize the value of effort more than ever. Without effort, there can be no business success, and without business success we cannot secure the money that is necessary to have in order to meet such people as you have been coming in contact with since you have been East. I do not expect to be in the game very much longer and it will be necessary for you younger men in the organization to work hard if this business is to continue to be successful and pay dividends as it has for the last thirty years.*

In 1932, Walter gained an additional temporary task that was brought on by the Depression, which he described in a letter to Helen. He was appointed to a federal emergency relief committee, which was responsible for finding community jobs for the unemployed, paying them $4 a day in food, clothing, fuel and medical care using $60,000 in federal funds. He noted that:

> *Seventy-five men have been working around the university, cleaning up and leveling land, taking out boulders and trees and making a big playground... which will be used as a physical education laboratory in doing practical work...I have been doing my best to keep the new Grocery Department going and have regretted my time has been so split up. However this relief work is exceedingly necessary at this time and Father seems to want me to do what I can to help.*

He added that the rearrangement of the grocery department had caused some consternation on the part of his father, adding that "at some considerable cost" it had to be redone because "Father was so dissatisfied with it."

Walter's first significant responsibility was actually the reconstruction of the Florence Hotel, which was across from the Mercantile on Higgins Avenue. It burned in 1936 for the second time, and C.H. was determined to rebuild the hotel for the benefit of the Missoula community (and, of course, the Mercantile).

Reportedly, C.H. did not hesitate in the decision to rebuild. With Walter in tow, they went up and down Higgins, soliciting financial support from

Firefighters protecting the Missoula Mercantile from rogue flames from a fire across the street at the Florence Hotel in 1936. *No. 86-0018, Archives and Special Collections, Mansfield Library, University of Montana.*

Photograph of a party celebrating the reopening of the Florence Hotel. Walter and C.H. McLeod are in front next to their wives. *No. 84-0041, Archives and Special Collections, Mansfield Library, University of Montana.*

Missoula businesses so that they would become part of the project. Involving the community proved to be a successful strategy. The major funding came, not surprisingly, from the Mercantile, but generous contributions were obtained from the Anaconda Company and Montana Power, as well as various members of the Hammond family, who then wanted participation in the decisions. The redwood for the Redwood Room, for example, came from the Hammond Lumber Company in California. Walter's suggestion of installing a large portrait in the lobby of Florence Hammond, for whom the hotel was named, was, however, nixed by her daughters. The important point here was that Walter not only had the job of choosing and overseeing the contractors but also of keeping good relations amongst the family members. Walter also extensively researched other hotels, looking for the best features to incorporate in order to make the new hotel as modern as possible. Ultimately, his efforts were successful, and the hotel opened to a grand reception in June 1941 that was attended by many out-of-town guests. Walter's limelight was temporarily overshadowed, however, by three circumstances involving his father: he had to take an exhausted C.H. to the Mayo Clinic in Rochester, Minnesota, for a "check-up," followed by C.H.'s subsequent illness and then his father's decision to resign.

A Difference in Style

To Walter, C.H.'s style may have been picky at times, but C.H. had certainly managed to keep the store profitable, even in difficult times of the Depression. In a letter written in the spring of 1941 to L.J. Bauer, who at that time was running a store in Columbia Falls where the Missoula Mercantile had partial interest, C.H. noted, "Our business in Missoula is keeping up very well; last month showed an increase of 19 percent over the same month a year ago and our sales for the year have increased 16 percent over the same period in 1940." He attributed the store's success to the construction and public works going on in Missoula at the time, but it certainly also had something to do with his management of MMCo.

Walter's management style would be quite different. He came to rely on a cadre of managers to handle the day-to-day business, and he became a member of several national boards, which kept him out of the store for weeks at a time. Walter bought a small ranch on the edge of Missoula in Orchard Homes and moved there around 1945. C.H. expressed his concern to his sister in a letter:

> *Walter has a big job on his hands—although I do not give him any advice—he is old enough to know what he wants to do, but he should not do anything that will take too much of his time from the business of the Missoula Mercantile Company. It is a big institution and last year its sales amounted to 8 million dollars.*

Walter was fifty-eight years old when this letter was written.

One of the first things that Walter did when he took hold of the reins was to seek and then take the advice of his brother-in-law, Dudley Richards, who was in advertising at Sears and Roebuck in Chicago. Walter felt it was time to hire a strong sales promotion and advertising man, and his correspondence with a potential candidate shows the differences in management styles, as well as the store's situation in late 1941:

> *Practically all our managers and buyers began their business careers with this company, starting out as young people. They have operated more or less independently though the years, under the direct supervision of my Father, and have never worked with anyone as I have proposed they shall work with you... This store is run differently than any institution in the United States...we have not followed the generally accepted methods of procedure that all of the larger stores that I know have—that is, having Merchandise Managers, detailed accounting systems for each department and so forth. My Father always felt that if we watched our stocks carefully, that a Merchandise Manager was not particularly necessary and we feel too that our business is not large enough to handle the great expense of a specialized, detailed accounting for each department.*

Walter pointed out that there were advertising handicaps in the Mercantile Company due to the simultaneous running of both the large wholesale hardware and grocery businesses and the retail business, given "the large number of wholesale customers we have in Western Montana." This dual wholesale-retail approach had been at the heart of the Missoula Mercantile's business since its beginning.

Walter struggled with the change. Writing in 1941 to his cousin, George McLeod, Walter expressed his vision:

Shoe department, 1940s. *No. 78-0050, Archives and Special Collections, Mansfield Library, University of Montana.*

It has always been a dream of mine that a much closer contact could be had between the management of our company and our employees, in spite of the fact that my Father has been unusually successful in maintaining a very harmonious relationship.

There were many factors affecting the store outside the purview of the Mercantile's control, most significantly the looming war, and Walter was quite aware of the likely effect on Missoula of losing workmen to the defense industry on the coast and of men going into the army, as well as the increased taxes to support the war effort. He observed, however, that the fertile agricultural land surrounding Missoula might be beneficial in the long run as war industries would dry up after the war. Competition from JC Penney and Montgomery Ward had not been a problem so far, as the Mercantile had emphasized the "better and popular priced lines," but Walter recognized that in the future, when people had less to spend, the Mercantile Company would have to compete in the lower-priced lines. Nonetheless, in December 1942,

Window display promoting sewing, 1950s. *No. 78-0070, Archives and Special Collections, Mansfield Library, University of Montana.*

he quietly dispatched Missoula Mercantile's legal counsel, George Shepard, to Washington to try to secure a government training program for eighteen- to nineteen-year-olds to bring more young men to Missoula.

> *Because Missoula has been so stripped of workmen and because the University will be in a tough spot if the large majority of boys were moved away...we feel it incumbent upon us to make a vigorous attempt to secure some project for Missoula which will keep the town reasonably well stimulated. The feeding of 1,290-2,000 would be a great benefit to the community.*

It was a successful effort, and a program was set up at the university.

Under Walter's watch, the Mercantile's community role, in many smaller ways, continued to be strong. The Mercantile supported the American Legion's junior basketball program, and Walter chaired the Red Cross drive, helped find space for the American Women's Voluntary Services and permitted the 4-H boys and girls to keep their animals in the Mercantile's garage during the 4-H club show, in spite of the fact that it "disorganized our trucking department to a considerable extent."

No doubt, this was an understatement. The list of contributions and dues for 1950 included over thirty donations and varied from Sanders County Hospital to the Montana State University track meet and the Missoula Lions Club Charity Horse Show.

Walter continued his father's commitment to the Boy Scouts and, in his own right, would become president of the Western Montana Council of the Boy Scouts of America. The council granted him the Silver Beaver Award, its highest award for an adult.

Effects of the War

The extensive U.S. involvement in World War II affected the running of the store in ways that were different from the situation C.H. had faced in World War I. Walter's letters contain numerous references to the difficulties of running the store, with prices fixed on many items, higher taxes and the lack of many staples that the Mercantile sold and that would not be available again until the end of the war. Some smaller issues illustrate this situation as well.

A memo dated December 3, 1942, addressed deliveries, noting that deliveries had been "radically curtailed in the interests of saving gas and rubber," so salespeople were to no longer ask the customer, "Do you wish to have this purchase delivered?" but were to ask, "Will you take the package with you?" instead. The memo concluded with the comment, "We wish to remind you how very few stores in Missoula have a delivery at all except for large bundles and bulky merchandise," indicating that the Mercantile was still trying to maintain a different level of service than other stores in Missoula in spite of the war.

In another 1942 bulletin, the need for a lunchroom was discussed. One had not previously existed, but due to rationing, employees had started bringing their lunches. Following this, a place for lunch was set up in the Express Company Room of the Rankin Block across Front Street from the Mercantile's main building, and it included hot plates, tea and coffee-making equipment. Soon, however, a cook who made a hot meal at lunchtime was hired, and the lunchroom was moved into a space in the department store itself, the location of which is still evident today. Mrs. Paloma Dahlstrom managed the lunchroom for many years, and while

Furniture department across the street from the main store, late 1940s. *No. 001-VIII_78-07_102, Archives and Special Collections, Mansfield Library, University of Montana.*

the room was primarily for the employees, family members sometimes ate there. Unlike many other department stores, the Missoula Mercantile never had a coffee shop or tearoom within the store. When the Florence Hotel reopened in 1941, it was able to serve that purpose, and there was no need for an additional restaurant.

A Changing Store: We Are Not Selling Out

After World War II, there was a general push in department stores across the country to revamp their appearance and provide a fresh look. Publications like *Planning the Post War Sporting Goods Department*

Above: Remodeled sporting goods department, 1950. *No. 001-VIII_78-07_102, Archives and Special Collections, Mansfield Library, University of Montana.*

Left: Women's lingerie, 1950. *No. 76-0104, Archives and Special Collections, Mansfield Library, University of Montana.*

New Hostess Shop and specialty gifts, 1950s. *The Macy's Collection, 2010.003. Used by Permission. All Rights Reserved.*

were not uncommon. The Missoula Mercantile hired a consultant to recommend changes to the store. It was during this process that the Mercantile Company determined not to tear down the store and build it again due to the prohibitive expense, but rather, in 1949, to undertake some reorganization of the existing store. At that time, there were 365 employees working for the Missoula Mercantile, 254 of whom worked in the retail part of the main store. Over $165,000 was projected to update and change various departments, with the largest expenditure ($43,984) on modernizing the ready-to-wear department.

Whether the reorganized store was better is a matter of perspective, but the times were different and seemed to demand different solutions. The store was determined to put on a new front. A full-page color ad in the 1950 yearbook of the Montana State University illustrates this, highlighted by the word "Progress!" and surrounded by photos of the new upgraded departments. A new brochure with these same photos was made available to customers.

The store tried to respond more to new customer demands. It created the new sportswear section in the women's fashion department, for example. Mrs. G. Webster of Missoula won the contest to name it. The name "Town and Country Shop" was chosen out of 254 entries in 1950. The Ski Shack was added to meet new demands in outdoor recreation. Merchandising plans were made out for each department; department managers were no longer left to design their departments. There was a greater emphasis on training. A training library was set up, and the department heads were encouraged to partake of its contents, which covered subjects from hosiery salesmanship to the National Retail Dry Goods Association Manual for Selling Shoes and educational aids for selling Manchester sterling flatware. Rules from "our instruction book" were discussed in weekly bulletins, most of which were updates of the early 1913 version.

Some of the less profitable departments disappeared. By 1950, the Missoula Mercantile had gone out of the retail grocery business, although the wholesale grocery business, which had been the core of the store's business since the beginning in 1866, still remained. The retail grocery business had been undercut by the success of the Red and White Grocery Stores, which the Missoula Mercantile had been influential in establishing.

Walter Outside the Store

In spite of all the change, Walter was not as tied to the store as his father had been and, indeed, spent considerable time away from it. Some such periods were unintentional, as he had several serious illnesses, but after his father retired in 1941, he became part of several national boards. Initially, however, his outside commitments related to the Missoula Mercantile.

In 1941, Walter was made a director of the Hammond Lumber Company, continuing the intertwining ownerships of Hammond interests that had made the Mercantile so successful. The next year, he added presidency of the Kalispell Mercantile (along with its Feed Grain Company, the Missoula Feed Grain Company and wholesale grocery department) to his interests.

Walter McLeod's business abilities were soon recognized outside of the company. In 1948, he was asked to be a director of the Northern Pacific Railroad, cementing a multiyear relationship between the Missoula Mercantile and the Northern Pacific, which went way back to the initial contract that Hammond had secured before the railroad's construction had reached Missoula. Thus, Walter must have been glad to be on the board.

In 1949, Northern Pacific directors took a four-thousand-mile trip from St. Paul to the West Coast to inspect the ten-year improvement program of the line designed to aid the growth of the economy of western Montana, as well as the railroad. The board had never stopped in Missoula before, and McLeod proudly served as master of ceremonies for a dinner for the fifteen-member board and one hundred plus Missoula businessmen in the Missoula Country Club. Walter continued as director of Northern Pacific until 1961.

Walter was also tapped as a member of the prestigious Federal Reserve Board of Minneapolis, a position he held from 1948 to 1950. He was a director of the Montana Power Company from 1955 to 1962. Walter also belonged to the exclusive club Rancheros Visitadores of Santa Barbara, California, and spent several vacations at that ranch with fellow businessmen from all over the country. It was a "diversion" he thoroughly enjoyed, and he also brought several of his friends into the club as members.

Restructuring the Corporation

Finally, one of the more significant things that occurred in the early 1950s thanks to Walter was a restructuring of the corporation, something that, of course, did not directly affect the customers. But for the reader today, it illustrates the extent to which the Missoula Mercantile was still deeply involved in western Montana when Walter took over.

Walter's restructuring effectively folded the Eddy Hammond & Company of Delaware, which Hammond had created in 1885 as a holding company for the Mercantile, into the Missoula Mercantile Company as a single corporation, thus creating a simpler structure. A plan of reorganization was submitted to the IRS in 1950 to set this change in motion. What is interesting here is to note the scope of the affiliated corporations that continued to be part of the Missoula Mercantile's operations. It is not necessary to go into detail, but they included not only the Florence Hotel, the South Missoula Land Corporation and one thousand shares of the Helena and Livingston Smelting and Refining Company but also nine companies where Missoula Mercantile was listed as the parent corporation:

Beckwith Bros. [in St. Ignatius]
Bozeman Feed and Grain Company*
Business Properties Security Company
Demers Mercantile Company [74 percent owned in Arlee]
Hamilton Feed and Grain Company*
Kalispell Feed and Grain Company*
Kalispell Grocery Company
Kalispell Mercantile Company
Missoula Feed and Grain Company*

*Signifies inactive at the time

In addition, the IRS application noted stock worth over $140,000 in still other companies:

Gallatin Farmers Oil Company
Gallatin Service Company
Golden Glo Creamery [in Missoula]
Hotel Florence Company
Ronan State Bank
Western Montana Dairy Breeders Association

Walter recognized that there was increasing competition from chain stores and other department stores and that the Missoula Mercantile's ability to continue to operate on many fronts as had been possible in his father's day was no longer viable. Indeed, he may have asked himself how the Missoula Mercantile could continue to be involved in so many organizations when its cornerstone, the retail Missoula Mercantile store, was slipping behind.

His changes to that facility had begun to raise suspicions, such that he circulated a memo among the employees entitled "Our Store Is Your Store," dispelling the idea that the store was for sale.

> *Now in fairness to our customers who look upon the Mercantile as a truly Western Montana Institution, and, at a time when we are undertaking a long-term remodeling program involving drastic changes, we desire to correct any such false impressions once and for all…Changes in merchandising are constantly occurring and your store is merely trying to anticipate and meet these changes—we are not selling out…We are a Missoula institution and we intend to remain that way.*

Even with his senior managers now in place—Ken Egen as treasurer, Jim Meyers as "our merchandise man" and Ty Robinson as counsel—and with Louis Bunge as vice-president and various reorganizations underway, there was the growing reality that the retail store was not operating as it once had when the Missoula Mercantile had been the "Big Store that sells everything and everything the very best."

Chapter Ten

CLOSING A CHAPTER OF MONTANA HISTORY

First the Banks and Then the Branches

Walter emerged from the store's reorganization intent on making more changes to try to bring a new order to the entire Mercantile establishment. In 1948, Walter hired R.H. "Ty" Robinson, a bright young lawyer, to replace counselor George Shepard, who had been killed in an automobile accident. Robinson, whose recollections of Missoula Mercantile history are extraordinary, willingly shares stories of its past and his assignments as in-house lawyer today. He worked directly for the Missoula Mercantile from the time he graduated from law school until 1954, when he became one of the organizing partners in the Missoula law firm of Garlington Lohr and Robinson, where he is now senior counsel. However, he continued to work on Missoula Mercantile issues for many years with his firm, slowly unwinding the many businesses that Hammond and C.H. McLeod had worked to establish. This task was finally finished in the 1980s, almost fifty years after A.B. Hammond's death in 1934.

Originally, the branch stores had effectively tied the Missoula Mercantile to many developing communities in western Montana, and Hammond often found it useful to start a bank in the community as well, ensuring that customers' money also stayed close to his control. It was really the Mercantile Company that propped up these small local banks in Thompson Falls, Plains,

Troy, Whitefish and Kalispell. In the early 1950s, it was Robinson's job to arrange for the sale of these banks, all of which were sold to the employees who paid 5 percent down and the rest over time.

Next, Robinson had to dispose of the remaining sawmills in the Missoula Mercantile portfolio, including two in eastern Washington, as well as the ones in the Montana towns of Troy and Columbia Falls that the Mercantile owned or owned shares in. During this period, the Missoula Mercantile also divested itself of its smaller affiliated stores, such as those at St. Ignatius, Charlo, Pablo and Polson. They also were generally bought by the employees, who were required to put up some of the money while paying the rest over time.

Grain Elevators Are Hard to Sell

Another major piece of the sales process was the grain elevators, some of which had been bought as recently as the 1940s. However, many had not been new when purchased, and grain elevators do not weather well. Most were not in good condition and were hard to sell. Robinson was told, "If you can get fifty cents on the dollar, take it," but mostly, he related, all he could get was thirty cents on the dollar. In addition to ones in Missoula, Ravalli and Polson, the Missoula Mercantile owned large grain elevators close to the eastern grain fields in Great Falls and Bozeman. The company elevator in Bozeman still stands today, one of the few grain elevators built during the 1930s between Minneapolis and Seattle. It was built in 1933 out of wood, not cement. The Mercantile Company took a chance in a time of financial depression and drought, but taking that chance demonstrated its long-term faith in eastern Montana's grain market. The company sold the Bozeman elevator in 1956 to Walter Teslow, who had been the manager of the Missoula Mercantile's eastern division and had overseen its construction. The elevator is now recognized as a historic site and serves as an art gallery under the name of MISCO Mill Gallery (MISCO was the name of the Mercantile's grain business).

The MISCO grain elevator at Kalispell had burned in 1945 in what was described as one of the worst fires in Kalispell history. It was not rebuilt. The Ceretana Grain Elevator in Missoula, which was part of MISCO, also remains and is part of a historic district there today.

Wholesale Grocery Goes Next, Wholesale Hardware Hangs On

In April 1954, a more radical change occurred in the operation of the Missoula Mercantile. The company sold its wholesale grocery departments in both Missoula and Kalispell. Writing to Hammond's daughter, Florence, Walter said, "It was a very hard decision to make for the reason that some of our men had been with us throughout their lifetime and we have had many local customers who are disappointed."

Walter cited competition from chain stores and cooperatives as the cause, as well as the large amount of capital required to keep stock on hand and the slim margin of the grocery department's profit. Additionally, without the retail grocery store (which had been sold earlier), there was no financial support from the retail part of Mercantile Company. Wholesale grocery was sold to the Utah Wholesale Grocery Company of Salt Lake for close to $1.5 million. The new company did not take on the forty-six employees who had worked in the wholesale grocery department. Losing employees with many years of service was a problem that Walter struggled with, apparently without a solution.

The wholesale hardware business, as Walter described in 1953, was "in a state of confusion." Advocating for a merging of the Kalispell and Missoula wholesale hardware departments, he argued that this strategy was necessary to save the wholesale hardware, which he perceived to be the moneymaking operation of the company. By selling the wholesale grocery business, cash had been generated, and the MMCo was able to take on the hardware consolidation that Walter had envisioned. In June 1955, construction was started on a new 142,000-square-foot building that was to house both the Kalispell and Missoula wholesale hardware departments in Missoula. The building was located on Harker Avenue, a block and a half off a major thoroughfare, Russell Street. The wholesale hardware department that had been located in several floors of the main retail store, as well as in Kalispell, would no longer be an inefficient operation in this state-of-the-art building. The new building would have a track of the Northern Pacific running right alongside an inside loading dock, making it possible to unload or load up to seven freight cars at the same time. Less than two years later, in March 1957, this new building, which was designed by Missoula architect H.E. Kirkemo, had its grand opening. It was the second-largest building in Missoula after the new Missoula County High School (now Sentinel High School). It included a merchandise display case, a catalog department and conference rooms for laying out plans. The *Missoulian* noted that the building had a telephone system with an intercom, teletypewriter connection to manufacturers and photographic darkroom for the catalog and an interconnecting pneumatic tube system to the cashier. It also noted that some overstocked items from long ago did not make the move to the new building, including buggy rivets and bolts, large wooden mallets and round-head boiler rivets, the latter of which had been made obsolete by welded structural steel.

Selling the Store and Creating a New One

The main retail store, however, was also not producing well. After the Korean War in 1959, Walter wrote to the stockholders of the Missoula Mercantile Company laying out a bleak future:

> *Our building is very old and inadequate for our needs. The floors and the carpeting are wearing out and a heating plant will have to be installed within a year, which would be very costly. To make these improvements in an antiquated building, we believe would be a waste of money…Our present space and distribution of merchandise is not modern, nor can we make it so…to build a new building… would cost well over $1 million. A new building would have to be financed… it would mean loss of dividends for an indefinite number of years…the only alternative is to sell the main store while we have the opportunity.*

He noted that there was only one offer to buy the store, which he deemed far from satisfactory. He also noted that competition from large chains made it difficult to make a profit and that family-owned stores were "fading and being replaced." He proposed a sale that would include the building, the parking lot, fixtures and inventory of the retail store and the old stone warehouse and the machine shop. The name Missoula Mercantile would be included in the sale as well. However, the wholesale hardware department, the farm implement department, the Kalispell

The new Montana Mercantile store housed the old store's wholesale hardware department. Photo taken in 1957. *The Audrey Kremis Schultz Collection, 2005.062. Used by Permission. All Rights Reserved.*

Mercantile and the Florence Hotel could not be included, as they were not of interest to the Allied Department Stores Company of Seattle, which was the purchaser. These assets would remain with the stockholders. The sale was completed in 1959.

The board of directors nevertheless felt that there was a sufficient volume of business to retain the wholesale hardware department. The board's solution was to create a new organization, the Montana Mercantile Company, to house these remaining assets. An added feature of this name was that it included the "MM" of MMCo, the company's abbreviated name. The board reasoned the MM "has long been symbolic of the name of the Company in its operation." Thus even at this late date, the Missoula Mercantile was once again taking a chance on a new venture, even as it had to part with what had made it famous, its retail store. Initially, Walter was president and general manager of the new Montana Mercantile Corporation.

Railroad siding in Montana Mercantile. *The Audrey Kremis Schultz Collection, 2005.062.160. Used by Permission. All Rights Reserved.*

It was not long before the Montana Mercantile divested itself of one more piece of the old Missoula Mercantile: the farm implement business that was located at 221 East Front Street in Missoula and at 1023 East Idaho Street in Kalispell. It was sold to a newly formed company that distributed International Harvester machinery called the Western Montana Implement Company. It would operate in western Montana and northern Idaho. Vern P. Stoterau, the former head of the Montana Mercantile's implement department, was hired as the general manager.

Walter retired in 1962, just shy of his seventy-fifth birthday, and became chairman of the board of the Montana Mercantile. He was worn out and could not wait for the transition. He had spent many months searching for the "right" person to take over the wholesale hardware store responsibilities from him. Larry Smith, who was then the manager of the Sears and Roebuck store in Butte, Montana, was chosen as the new manager and became its president as well. At age fifty-eight, he would be in charge of not only the one hundred employees of the Montana Mercantile but also

Farm implement department. *No. 002-XXVI_015_ImplementsWrhs, Archives and Special Collections, Mansfield Library, University of Montana.*

the Kalispell Mercantile, a wholly owned subsidiary with fifty employees, and the Florence Hotel, of which the Montana Mercantile remained the major stockholder. There were no longer McLeods or Hammonds involved in the day-to-day management of any of the former Missoula Mercantile operations. They remained as stockholders, but the liquidation of the company was not far off.

The Demise of the Mercantile

When the Missoula retail store was sold in 1959 to Allied Department Stores, the name Missoula Mercantile was also sold, and most of the employees remained, including the then vice-president, James E. Meyers, who later became Allied's general manager. Now, instead of having McLeod as his boss, Meyers reported to a vice-president in Seattle who was head of Allied's western group (which included eighteen stores, at least two of which were called Bon Marché in Seattle and Spokane). A new controller from Seattle was placed in the Missoula store as well. On the outside of the building, the old name remained the same.

Allied did not make many changes in the next decade, but a rebuilding of the store that had been orally agreed on never materialized. Allied resisted attempts to move the store from downtown to the new mall that was being created after doing a study that indicated its stores did better to remain part of downtown. Southgate Mall would open in August 1978 without the Missoula Mercantile as an anchor of that operation.

Probably no one fully appreciated the significance of an ad in the March 26, 1978 edition of the *Missoulian.* The sponsor of the ad was "The Bon/ The Mercantile," and there was a small note that read, "Only our name is changing." Only a week before, the ad's sponsor had been "The Mercantile." By June, The Bon was the sole sponsor of the store's ads. The disappearance of the Missoula Mercantile went seemingly unnoticed, mostly because little fanfare was made of the change.

By becoming part of Allied Department stores, the Missoula Mercantile merged into a large corporate domain, and instead of controlling its branch stores and much of the markets in western Montana, the situation was reversed, and it had to go with the flow as dictated from a higher source (which was, at first, from Seattle but eventually from a new corporate headquarters in New York when Allied itself merged with Federated Department Stores).

The Bon Marché (named after the Paris store but with no relation to it) began as a department store in Seattle in 1890 and was started by the Norhoff family. Soon, there were several Bon Marché stores, and these stores were soon acquired by Allied Department Stores in 1929, which retained the name. It was a successful operation, and after the end of World War II, Allied added several more stores. The Missoula Mercantile was one of these additions, and it became a Bon Marché store, although there was no immediate rush to make all the stores carry the same name. In 1989, Allied was then merged into Federated Department Stores, which owned Macy's and Bloomingdale's and was based in New York. By 1992, the Bon Marché component of Allied Department Stores was fully incorporated with Federated.

From 1978, the Missoula store was known simply as The Bon, but it appeared to have added the "Marché" in the late 1980s to match the Seattle store. A *Missoulian* ad for The Bon Marché in 1998 used an old 1890s photo of the Missoula Mercantile Company and read: "Growing up with Missoula, Faithfully Serving Western Montana for 133 years." Even the old triangular MMC logo was part of the ad. A 1980s employee credit card carried the words "Bon Marche," but a customer card issued in the 1990s had "Marché." In August 2003, the corporate name was changed again to Bon-Macy's, but by January 2005, a new sign that read Macy's appeared on the outside of the Missoula store. In February 2008, the entire northwest department of Macy's was laid off in Seattle, and all of the former Bon Marché stores were put under Macy's western division in California. By early 2010, Macy's had closed many of these stores, including the retail store in Missoula. After a month of sales, the building was emptied and the lights turned off in January 2010.

This ownership of the later life of the Missoula Mercantile was sadly but necessarily limited by the fact that when Allied merged into Federated in 1989, its local records reportedly disappeared into the Missoula dump. Macy's, however, was persuaded to turn a significant number of remaining artifacts from the building over to the Historical Museum at Fort Missoula, and some of this collection is now part of a permanent exhibit about Missoula County at the Museum. Almost one hundred years of correspondence and records are, however, preserved at the K. Ross Toole Archives of the University of Montana, invaluable documents that describe the early history of the store, but a piece regarding the details of corporate ownership of the retail store after 1959 is still missing.

Bon Marché credit card. *Author's collection.*

Macy's exterior showing a portion of the one-hundred-foot display windows, 2010. *Copyright Alan Graham McQuillan.*

Eddy Hammond & Company original logo. *No 001-1_24-22 Archives and Special Collections, Mansfield Library, University of Montana.*

Some major pieces of Hammond's enterprises still remained for the stockholders of the Montana Mercantile Company to dispose of after Walter died in 1963: the wholesale hardware department, the Kalispell Mercantile and the Florence Hotel. It was not long before they sold the wholesale hardware department to the International Telephone and Telegraph Company. The Florence Hotel was also sold to a private owner, who converted it into offices and renamed it the Glacier Building. Likewise, the Kalispell Mercantile was sold, and it closed in 1980. However, four lots of the South Missoula Land Company remained, lots that had never been built on. It was not until the early 1980s that this last piece was completed.

Walter had written to each Missoula Mercantile employee before the sale of the retail store to Allied Department Stores in 1959, trying to explain what had happened. His words best describe his feelings:

> *To sell and leave the Missoula Mercantile Company with its long history as a building force in Western Montana was a difficult decision and caused me many months of heartache. My father came to Missoula in 1880, lived and worked in what is now the Men's Clothing Department, and was the only clerk. From that small beginning and under his management until his retirement in June 1941, the store grew to its present size, I have spent my lifetime with the Company and have tried to follow his policies; consequently it was like closing a chapter of Montana history.*

The building was acquired in 2011 by Octagon Partners, a Virginia-based investment firm that specializes in historic restoration, and the company enthusiastically aims to restore the building and put it to a new use. The firm wants to keep it a vibrant part of downtown, and this bodes well for Missoula. The new building, "the Historic Missoula Mercantile," will open a new chapter in Montana history.

Afterword

THE FUTURE OF THE HISTORIC MISSOULA MERCANTILE

The building that housed the Missoula Mercantile and the retail stores that followed is now on the verge of a new life. Some indications of this future have been made public, but most are still unannounced. But that story is beyond the scope of this history. It must be said, however, that Missoula and its citizens are looking forward to the reopening of their Missoula Mercantile and its future involvement with downtown Missoula.

Before leaving the story of the old Missoula Mercantile, it is perhaps interesting to see if the building itself has any stories to tell the future. With that in mind, we shall head to the basement, the least changed part of the store.

Exploring the Empty Basement

Once Macy's ended its closing sale and the liquidators moved out, there was seemingly nothing moveable in the two-and-a-half-story-high building covering thirty-three thousand square feet of Missoula's downtown area. One does not often get a chance to examine an empty department store. During the sale, it was hard to image what the building would be like without

The main floor's interior after Macy's closed the Missoula Mercantile building, 2011. *Copyright Alan Graham McQuillan.*

all the merchandise in it. Before that, the thought had not occurred. The merchandise, with its concentrated lighting, focused one's attention on just that—the merchandise—rather than the features of the building, such as the ornate tin ceilings or the creaking staircases. Of course, there was no customer access to the basement in its last few reincarnations of the store.

Octagon granted us permission to look at the building, and by the end of the tour, we realized that while it may appear empty, it is amazingly full of history and memory-joggers. Our tour guides included Steve McFaddon, who had been the maintenance manager for more than eighteen years, and Dennis Sain, now in his seventies and whose mother had worked in the shoe department in the 1950s. He and his brother would meet her there after elementary school and explore the building unaccompanied by adults. He later worked in the store in 1958 in the toy department.

Here's a sampling of the things we learned: which walls had been changed; which tin ceilings had been covered up by suspended ceilings; and how the mezzanines, added perhaps as late as the 1950s, created low spaces underneath that were difficult to use in a modern retail environment, especially when customers were taller.

Tin ceiling in the Missoula Mercantile building, 2011. *Copyright Alan Graham McQuillan.*

And because a sampling is not enough, here's a longer, more detailed list:

- The empty shaft that once held a dumbwaiter brought china up from the basement to the display area on the main floor.
- The freight elevator with its heavy latticed doors still functioned. It was the second one, having been built in 1934, and it had never been replaced or even broken down. Freight was unloaded here from the narrow alley by hand trucks (now in the Historical Museum). A forklift was only used during the last ten years of the store.
- The steam heat system reached the rooms by cast-iron radiators, which were probably made in a local foundry and carried from the steam plant next to the river close by. A.B. Hammond, unsurprisingly,

had once owned the steam plant and brought its heat to his four corner buildings: the Florence Hotel, the Hammond Building, the First National Bank and the Missoula Mercantile. Pipes are evident throughout the building. Eventually, a boiler fed by coal, and more recently a gas boiler, replaced the system. When steam was used, the Mercantile was charged by how much water went through the system, measured on the way out.

- Fire protection was achieved through the presence of bulky canvas hoses that were neatly folded into metal cages, which still remain attached to the walls. There was no sprinkler system until more recent years.
- It was easy to spot the shoe department and its accompanying storage area. Wooden shelves with size numbers neatly painted on them identified where to find size 7 ladies' shoes or men's boots. Work boots and clothing had been sold downstairs. In one corner of the shoe department, there once sat the shoe-fitting fluoroscope, made by Simplex in Wisconsin. It is now on display at the Historical Museum. Older readers will remember this machine allowed customers to see X-rays of their feet to see that the shoes fitted well, until the machines were banned in the 1950s for health reasons. Walter had urged his father to pay the $850 for what was, in 1927, thought to be an innovative machine and hardly something to be found in a western store.
- The last owners grossly underutilized the potential floor space, occupying only 60,000 square feet out of the available 113,000 square feet. Even when the store was the Missoula Mercantile, much of the space was used for storage rather than retail, something that is not as common in a modern retail store where storage is not as important and where inventory can be replenished quickly.
- Pneumatic tubes ran all over the building from the accounting department on the second floor to all departments, quickly transporting the cash in and bringing receipts and change back. The motor for the pneumatic system is still in the basement. The store, when it was still E.H. Hammond & Company, had been an early adopter of a version of a cash-boy system, which carried a cash box on metal wires hanging from the ceiling from the clerk to a central cashier who could check his figures and make change. In 1921, under C.H. McLeod, it was replaced at a cost of $11,000 by the pneumatic tubes, a system that operated by compressed air to carry the cash, which it did at a much greater speed. It was used until the 1960s, but many tubes remain.

Shoe-fitting fluoroscope. *From the Macy's Collection, 2010.003. Used by Permission. All Rights Reserved.*

As we headed downstairs, a short door appeared, part of the steam tunnel system. John Wayne reportedly used this particular door when he came to Missoula and stayed at the Florence Hotel in the 1950s. Walter McLeod let him shop after hours so that he could avoid detection by the crowds, and the door led to a tunnel that connected to the Florence Hotel across the street. This, like many others of Missoula's early tunnel system, is blocked off and filled in today. Downstairs we learned more:

- Early delivery of goods to customers was by horse- and mule-drawn wagons. The story goes that these animals were kept indoors at night in stalls in the basement, getting in and out by means of the freight elevator.
- The animals might have shared their accommodations on one occasion with some of the thirty-two carloads of circus animals from when the Ringling Brothers Circus came to town on August 7, 1909. There is no official record, but the story persists, and the words "Ringling Brothers 1909" are scrawled on a fire door and on columns in the basement.
- A section of the basement is also known for stories about a ghost, purportedly an older man with suspenders. Many contend that this is the ghost of Walter McLeod. It was well known that some of the women employees refused to go into the basement.
- Boards used for shelving were as wide as twenty inches, perhaps not unusual for the late 1800s, which was the era of large trees. (The boards would have been supplied by Hammond's lumber mill at nearby Bonner.) The beams in the basement ceiling are hefty, easily twelve by twelve feet in length. Some joists were rough-sawn and measured three by twelve feet, only slightly smaller than those the Bonner Mill made to hold up the mine shafts in Butte (thirteen by fourteen feet). Apparently, when the Missoula Mercantile decided to sell rugs on the floor above, an engineer reassured the store that the weight of heavy rugs would be just fine; the floor was so strong, they could drive a fleet of trucks over it.
- Many of the posts in the basement bear the scrawled names of employees, some of which were from as far back as the 1890s. One post records the years worked. Even Hammond's name appears, though there is no indication that it was he who actually placed it there. There are no signatures of the McLeods', but a box used for packing materials has many names, some in English and others in Japanese. The box is a relic that will be preserved by the new owners, as well as the names on the posts.
- A modern chute coming down from the unloading dock above was the first step for sorting boxes off the trucks. Each box was then carried to

Ringling Brothers Circus announcement on a post, 2011. *Copyright Alan Graham McQuillan.*

Circus parade in front of the Missoula Mercantile, circa 1909. *Pictorial Histories Publishing Company.*

Years of service. Post in the Missoula Mercantile basement, 2011. *Copyright Alan Graham McQuillan.*

a nearby area designated for a specific department, where a cadre of employees folded or put on hangers what was in the boxes. This was the system used in the 1960s.

- A yellow arrow on the floor indicated the way to the electronics department, a department that appeared in the basement in the late 1950s and continued into the 1980s.
- Measurements on the floor and a worn post are remnants of the area where rope was measured out.
- A line of hooks on a beam shows where buggy whips once hung. They were sorted by size before the later days when they were confined to a barrel.
- Whiskey barrels were stored in one of the stone areas of the basement. Reportedly, when farmers came in to pay their yearly bill in the 1880s, they would be given a shot of whiskey.

And although not in the basement, we found some memories lurking on the second floor as well. There is a metal spiral staircase at the corner

Left: A post worn from measuring rope in the Missoula Mercantile basement, 2011. *Copyright Alan Graham McQuillan.*

Below: Liquor barrels in the basement of the Missoula Mercantile before 1890. *No. 084-0048, Archives and Special Collections, Mansfield Library, University of Montana.*

A spiral metal staircase to the roof from the second floor of the Missoula Mercantile building, 2011. *Copyright Alan Graham McQuillan.*

of what had been the office that led to a large room on the third floor and also gave access to the roof. The room held rows of shelves and was used for display storage and manikins. The freight elevator had access to this floor. It is not known whether it was originally designed for storage. Some employees had access to the roof, and many of the photos of parades on Higgins Avenue show people watching from the roof of the Missoula Mercantile. It was thought that it was the job of some to use the rooftop vantage to keep alert for enemy planes during World War II. Finally, the twelve-foot vault mentioned in chapter seven will remain on the second floor. It, too, was empty.

Musings on the Architecture

Staircases dominate the basement. Even with two closed off, there are still three remaining. It is easy to see the lines of the foundation walls as each new addition was completed along with its accompanying stairs. The Historic Preservation Certification Application that was prepared for the new owners cites the stone walls and brick arches in the basement as "a character-defining feature of the Mercantile." That the elevations change slightly between additions does not seem to have affected the building's solid durability. Wooden floors were added over the concrete so as to make walking easier for customers and salespeople. It is impressive to realize that the basic footprint of the store, which was established within eight years of breaking ground, is still the same today.

The exterior of the Missoula Mercantile has also changed significantly over the building's more than one hundred years of existence. Its brick and stone presence on the corner of Higgins and Front was a stark change from Eddy and Hammond's log cabin on West Front, certainly a solid indication that the store was here to stay. Thanks to the extensive historical architectural survey done for the new owners of the building, there is a much better understanding now of the changes that have taken place. Our architectural musings are aided by this new information.

The oldest part of the building is the southwest end. Old basement walls, believed to be part of the original 1877 store, were uncovered about seven feet from the curb along Higgins when Montana Power Company was replacing

One of five staircases in the basement of the Missoula Mercantile building, 2011. *Copyright Alan Graham McQuillan.*

Original stone foundations visible in the basement, 2011. *Copyright Alan Graham McQuillan.*

water mains in 1949. Additions to the original store were made several times as increasing business demanded more space. By 1884, a second floor over a portion of the store was added for offices, and before too long, it covered the whole of the building. An 1890 Sanborn Insurance map notes that openings along the alley were to be closed with iron shutters for fire protection, and these features are still visible today.

A striking change occurred along Higgins Avenue in 1905 when the Missoula Mercantile turned the building's west-facing side (in its words, "a dull and unattractive brick wall" that had long been used for advertising) into a one-hundred-foot, Art Nouveau–inspired showcase window.

Around 1915, the storefront was further enhanced by the installation of "Luxfer prism glass" over the new display windows. Using prisms, these windows would redirect light into darker spaces to the rear of the store, thereby cutting down on the need for artificial lighting. This innovation had been patented as early as 1896. Glass blocks on the second floor were also used to bringing light from skylights. A striking copper Art Nouveau entrance

A glass block on the second floor of the Missoula Mercantile building, 2011. *Copyright Alan Graham McQuillan.*

An artist's illustration of the Missoula Mercantile Company as the Bon, circa 2000. *The Macy's Collection, 2010.003. Used by Permission. All Rights Reserved.*

canopy was most likely added that year, making official the reorientation of the store from its original Front Street entrances to one fronting on Higgins Avenue, becoming the main door. Both the huge display windows and the door canopy still remain today.

In 1949, two doors along Front Street that led to the dry goods and shoe departments were removed and replaced with plain windows. Originally, all the departments had their own doors on East Front, and it is still possible to see the metal door stoops and accompanying iron columns that were built around 1888. The name on the columns is Mesker Brothers of St. Louis, Missouri, a company that had specialized since 1846 as an iron store and also sold house fronts.

The building has not always been red brick, although before 1924, it was painted red to enhance the red brick. The store was painted white before 1924 and remained so until the 1970s, when the paint was sandblasted off to expose the red brick. This, however, caused much damage to the soft Missoula bricks.

The large windows upstairs that looked out on Higgins Avenue and Front Street were also bricked up in the 1970s, as were all the second-floor windows along the long side of Higgins Avenue. This was to allow for more interior merchandise display space, although the outlines of the windows are clearly visible, and if Octagon's plans are approved, the large windows will be restored.

We do not know much about the men who built the building, hauled the large stones for the foundations and heaved the huge beams into place. There are no existing architectural drawings, nor is it known if there were any. It is, nonetheless, a well-built structure that has lasted well over one hundred years, and its future now looks promising as a mixed retail, office and restaurant space.

NOTE TO THE READER

All correspondence quoted in this book can be found in the K. Ross Toole Archives of the University of Montana in Missoula, Montana. Most of what is reprinted here is from the C.H. McLeod (001) and Walter H. McCleod (002) collections.

If you have stories or artifacts from the Missoula Mercantile, the Historical Museum at Fort Missoula would be interested in hearing from you. Please contact them at: Historical Museum at Fort Missoula, 322 Fort Missoula, Missoula, Montana 59804, or e-mail them at ftmslamuseum@montana.com.

REFERENCES

Archives and Special Collections, Mansfield Library, University of Montana–Missoula

My main sources were the correspondence, related files and photographs of the two store managers, Charles H. and Walter McLeod, which are part of the University of Montana Archives and Special Collections. In addition, C.H. McLeod's collection contained correspondence from A.B. Hammond that was supplemented by the two excellent PhD theses on Hammond by Dale Johnson and Greg Gordon. The detailed files of Audra Browman on Missoula's early history, including her incredible card files on early newspapers, were also a great help. The photography collections available at the archives were a great source of photos, and the oral histories were invaluable.

Specifically, these resources included: Charles Herbert McLeod Papers, Mss. 001; Walter Herbert McLeod Papers, Mss. 002; and Audra Arnold Browman Papers, Mss. 468 (esp. Series VI: Research Card Files). The photographic collections used include: R.H. McKay Photographs, Mss. 249; Edward H. Boos Photographs, Mss. 346 and Mss. 672; John Dunn Photographs, Mss. 361; and Stan Healy Photographs, Mss. 430. Oral histories consulted include: 051 Tom Haines; 0124 James E. Meyers; 0131-19 Jack Beckwith; 0396 Ty Robinson; and 0415-01 Ty Robinson.

Other articles and books within the archives that were consulted are: George B. McLeod, "The Story of the Hammond Lumber Company," interview by David Way, 1953, CRA, typescript, Walter H. McLeod Papers, Mss. 002, Series XIV Box 96 Folder 4; Lloyd Zimmerman, *The Missoula Mercantile Company* (Missoula, MT: 1962) and Kalispell Mercantile Company Catalog (Kalispell, MT: Kalispell Mercantile Company, 1919?). Two theses on A.B. Hammond were also used: Greg Gordon, "Money Does Grow on Trees: A.B. Hammond and the Age of the Lumber Baron" (PhD diss., University of Montana, 2010); and Dale L. Johnson, "Andrew B. Hammond: Education of a Capitalist on the Montana Frontier" (PhD diss., University of Montana, 1976).

Early Histories

These resources provided the background for Montana's early history. The most useful references were the following: Albert Partoll, *St. Michael's: Montana's Pioneer Church* (Missoula, MT: Exchange Club, 1962); Bureau of Census, Montanta for the years 1870, 1880 and 1900, Ancestry.com, June 26, 2012, www.ancestry.com; George F. Weisel, *Men and Trade on the Northwest Frontier* (Missoula: Montana State University Press, 1955); Henry Pickering Walker, *The Wagonmasters* (Norman: University of Oklahoma, 1966); Joaquin Miller, *An Illustrated History of the State of Montana* (Chicago: Lewis Publishing, 1894); John H. Beadle, *The Undeveloped West: Or, Five Years in the Territories* (Philadelphia, PA: National Publishing Company, 1873), Google e-book, 2008; M.A. Leeson, *History of Montana, 1739–1885* (Chicago: 1885); Patrice Schwenk and the Loyola Sacred Heart High School Historical Research Class, *Sisters of Providence: The Missoula Mission, 1873–1923* (Missoula, MT: Historical Museum at Fort Missoula, 2008); and Roberta Cheney, *Names on the Faces of Montana* (Missoula, MT: Mountain Press Publishing, 1984).

Historic Registration and Certification

Both the Missoula Mercantile and one of its warehouses are listed on the National Register of Historic Places, so their registration forms were consulted: Missoula Downtown Historic District, 1990, and Missoula Mercantile Warehouse, 2004. New architectural information about the building was obtained from a Historic Preservation Certification Application prepared by CTA Architects for the owners (October 4, 2012).

Missoula's Historic Resources

These valuable resources include: Allan James Mathews, *A Guide to Historic Missoula* (Helena: Montana Historical Society, 2002); James R. McDonald, *Missoula Historic Resource Survey* (Missoula, MT: Historic Research Associates, 1980); Jo Rainbolt, *Missoula Valley History* (Dallas, TX: Curtis Media, 1991); John H. Toole, *Red Ribbons: A Story of Missoula and Its Newspaper* (Davenport, IA: Lee Enterprises, 1989); Lenora Koelbel, *Missoula: The Way It Was* (Missoula, MT: Gateway Printing, 1972); "Missoula-Hellgate Centennial 1860–1960" (Missoula, MT: Missoula-Hellgate Centennial Committee, 1960); Missoula County Historic Preservation Commission Office (attributed to), *Historical Significance of the Missoula Mercantile and Its Founders* (Missoula, MT: n.d.); Ruth Boydston Scott, *Missoula: Trading Post to Metropolis,* vol. 1 and 2 (Missoula, MT: 1977); Sanborn Insurance Maps, Missoula 1884–1921, available online through Missoula County Historic Preservation Office; and Shirley Jay Coon, "The Economic Development of Missoula Montana" (PhD diss., University of Chicago, 1926). Over two hundred items from the Missoula Mercantile are archived at the Historical Museum at Fort Missoula.

Oral Histories Conducted by Author with Former Employees

Much valuable information was garnered talking with these wonderful folks: Judy Baldizar; Ty Robinson; Debra Wold McConaughey; Steve McFaddon; Gordon and Ina Swanson; Dennis and Anna Sain; Hope Stocksted; and Chris Roholt, who interviewed his ninety-year-old mother, Sophronia Beagle Roholt, about her employment at the Mercantile. Except for the oral histories mentioned above, these are in the author's collection.

Community Histories

Many communities compiled histories during the U.S. Bicentennial, and these provided good information about the branch stores. Sources included: Bicentennial Committee, Bonner School, *A Grassroots Tribute: The Story of Bonner, Montana* (Bonner, MT: Bonner School, 1976); Bitter Root Valley Historical Society, *Bitterroot Trails III* (Stevensville, MT: Stonydale Press, 1998); Frenchtown Historical Society, *Frenchtown Valley Footprints* (Frenchtown, MT: 1976); Jeffrey H. Langton, *The Victor Story: History of a Bitterroot Valley Town* (Missoula, MT: Pictorial Histories, 1985); Kathryn L. McKay, *A Guide to Historic Kalispell* (Helen: Montana Historical Society Press, 2001); Kathryn L. McKay; *Looking Back: A Pictorial History of the Flathead Valley, Montana* (Kalispell: Northwest Montana Historical Society, 1997); Olive Wehr and the St. Ignatius Senior Citizens, *The Heritage of Mission Valley* (St. Ignatius, MT: Mission Valley News, 1975); and Stevensville Historical Society, *Montana Genesis: A History of the Stevensville Area of the Bitterroot Valley* (Missoula, MT: 1971).

Newspapers and References

The Missoula newspapers (the *Missoula Gazette* and *Missoulian*) on microfilm at the Missoula Public Library (MPL) provided information on parts of the Missoula Mercantile's early history. The *Missoulian*'s bicentennial edition (1976) was particularly useful. The MPL's set of Polk City directories was also invaluable. These include: *Missoula Gazette*, 1888–90; *Missoulian*, 1880; *Missoulian*, July 2, 1976, bicentennial edition; *Missoulian-Sentinel*, July 27, 1960, centennial edition; and various Polk City directories from 1900.

INDEX

N

ABOUT THE AUTHOR

After a career in land conservation in Maine, Minie moved to Missoula, Montana, where she researched and wrote exhibit scripts for the County Historical Museum, including one for the award-winning exhibit on the Great Fire of 1910. She and an associate started a local history center to preserve stories and artifacts of a community near Missoula that, for over one hundred years, supported a lumber mill and hydroelectric dam. Both are now gone. In 2012, she received the Missoula Historic Preservation Commission's Dorothy Ogg Award for individual contribution in the city/county division. She lives in Missoula with her husband, whose photographs are included in this book.

Visit us at
www.historypress.net